The Landlord's Guide to LETTING

The Landlord's Guide to LETTING

How to buy and let residential property for profit

Moira Stewart

howto**books**

Published by How To Books Ltd,
3 Newtec Place, Magdalen Road,
Oxford OX4 1RE, United Kingdom.
Tel: (01865) 793806. Fax: (01865) 248780.
email: info@howtobooks.co.uk
http://www.howtobooks.co.uk

Second edition 1999
Reprinted 2000
Reprinted with amendments 2001
Reprinted 2002 (twice)
Reprinted 2003
Third edition 2005

British Library Cataloguing in Publication Data.
A catalogue record for this book is available from
the British Library.

Produced for How To Books by Deer Park Productions, Tavistock
Cover design by Basline Arts Ltd, Oxford
Typeset by PDQ Typesetting, Stoke-on-Trent, Staffs.
Printed and bound by Cromwell Press, Trowbridge, Wiltshire

Contents

List of Illustrations

Preface

to the Third Edition

Many have the chance to become a landlord, yet few realise the potential. Some are held back by factors such as inexperience, lack of confidence or an inability to see themselves in the role. Some may even think that owning a property is a prerequisite. Not so! Now in its third edition this book explains that the essentials necessary to become a landlord are very few indeed, and aims to give everyone the chance to consider letting as an option open to them.

Let me immediately explain that the use of the term 'landlord' throughout this book has no basis in gender preference. Rather it is because the constant use of 'landlord or landlady' and the accompanying terms 'he or she' and 'him or her' would very quickly become clumsy. Those who let property can be either sex, be from any adult age group, come from any part of the country, from any background, education, race or social sector. Within this book the term 'landlord' may even encompass a couple or group of joint partners.

While most books look at letting from the tenant's perspective, this book considers the *landlord's* choices, obligations, duties and rights. It highlights important decisions, lists practical tips and offers the reader an opportunity to assess his or her own letting situation. Recently updated, this third edition provides current information on legislation and taxation.

Society hasn't always held landlords in the highest regard, but being a landlord is a respectable way to engage in business and a landlord who performs his duties well has every right to take pride in his actions and achievements. I hope this book will provide all the information, inspiration and confidence required for *you* to become a successful landlord!

This book is dedicated to my son, Ian, whose zest for life is my inspiration.

Moira Stewart

Getting Started

Being a landlord is not just about owning property. A landlord is a businessman, his let is a business venture and his objective is to run an efficient and profitable service. The main prerequisite to becoming a landlord, therefore, is a sound assessment of:

a. investment potential
b. risk
c. personal skills and capabilities.

DECIDING TO BECOME A LANDLORD

As a first step, ask yourself the following questions:

- ◆ Do I have some spare time?
- ◆ Am I ready to seek out facts and information?
- ◆ Am I prepared to accept responsibility on issues of safety?
- ◆ Am I willing to consult others for advice?
- ◆ Am I prepared to accept an element of risk involved in making a business deal?

If you can answer 'yes' to *all* these questions, you have taken a step towards becoming a landlord.

Identifying your personal skills

Being a landlord does not mean you have to undertake the

day-to-day letting workload yourself. You can employ someone else to do it for you; but if you choose to do some or most of the letting duties yourself, you will need to be able to:

- communicate with others
- organise effectively
- behave assertively
- respond to new situations
- stick to rules and guidelines.

Beginning the learning process

As a preliminary to letting, you must:

- Understand an assessment of the profitability of your planned let.
- Be aware of your legal obligations as a landlord, especially with regard to safety issues.
- Be aware of the two types of taxation you will encounter in letting.
- Know when and where to get advice and how to choose an adviser.

Making a start

You have already made a start by reading this far! By continuing with this chapter you will:

1. Become aware of factors which affect profitability.

2. Begin to think about your own situation and start to make plans.

3. Make an initial assessment of the profit potential of your own proposed let.

The chapters which follow will lead you through the whole letting process.

LOOKING AT PROFIT AND RISK

There are two types of profit to be made from letting property:

- capital profit
- income profit.

Both have to be considered carefully in assessing overall profitability. The difficulty is that neither is possible to predict with certainty. There are always going to be assumptions and guesswork in your forward planning calculations and this translates into an element of risk in the venture as a whole. There are steps you can take towards minimising these risks, of course, but only you can ultimately decide if the risk level can be reduced enough to be acceptable to you.

Understanding capital profit

The financial gain you make between the buying and selling price of your property is your capital profit and may well play a significant part in assessing your overall profitability. It is, of course, always possible to make a loss as nothing is certain! There are also expenses (buying and selling costs and taxation) which may eat into your capital profit, reducing it significantly.

On the whole however, property has been recognised as having good long-term investment potential. Figure 1 shows the dramatic rise in house prices over a 30 year period. An average house purchased for £25,000 in 1980

could have been sold ten years later for over £68,000. A
return of over 270 per cent! Only ventures on the stock
market could have equalled such gain, and like stock
market investments, property investment carries with it an
element of risk. Past performance is not a guarantee of
future performance.

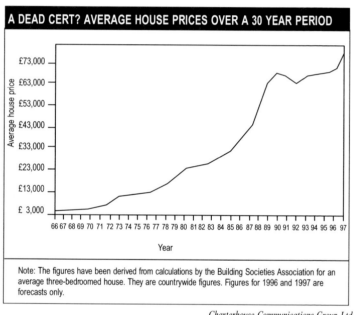

Charterhouse Communications Group Ltd.

Fig. 1. Average house prices over a 30 year period.

Knowing when to buy and sell

The housing market goes through cycles. It is liable to
have spells where buyers are few and prices are depressed.
It is equally likely to have times when everyone wants to
buy and prices soar. This is excellent news for the investor:
buy in the slump and sell at the peak is the obvious advice
to follow.

Property prices vary regionally, the south-east of England being recognised as the most expensive area, with London hitting the highspot. The local economic climate within the area of his or her proposed investment can be of greater significance to the investor, however. Each local area, as well as following the national trend, will have its own economic sub-climate and it is important to be aware of what powers the local economy and what may affect it.

Getting the timing right
In order to buy and sell advantageously, timing is all-important. There are a number of indicators that will help you to decide when you should buy or sell your property.

1. The national economic trend. A depressed national economy depresses the housing market and sends out a buy signal, timed to best advantage just as the economy begins an upward swing. A buoyant economy stimulates the housing market and sends out a sell signal.

2. The local economic sub-climate. This works in exactly the same way as the national economic trend. Local trends are often stronger than national ones and may swamp any national signals.

3. Follow London. Changes in the housing market often start in London and the south-east and ripple outwards. This can give you an advance warning of changes coming your way, assuming your property is outside London, but remember that any national trend may not be enough to buck any strong local economic factor.

4. Movement starts from the bottom up. The cheap end of the housing market nearly always starts to move first after a slump. The movement ripples progressively up into the more expensive housing levels. This is usually true for any geographical area and is a signal well worth watching for.

Weighing up warnings over an impending slump in property values
The national news regularly features headlines informing us of the trend in house price values, usually when quarterly figures have just been released. These often attract most attention when the immediate trend is downwards and analysts express opinions as to whether this heralds a downwards spiral.

An investor must make up his own mind on which analyst to believe but remember that property investment is a long-term venture and it is the overall trend, and not the short-term fluctuations, which is important. Figure 2 shows the recent trend in average house price across the whole of the UK. The figures have been sourced from the Office of the Deputy Prime Minister where there are further statistics available on a regional basis. (See Useful Web Sites section.)

Minimising the risk to your capital profit
◆ Know your property market. Spend time following the market over a period of time.

◆ Be prepared to wait. Try to have enough flexibility in your finances to allow you to wait for the right economic climate.

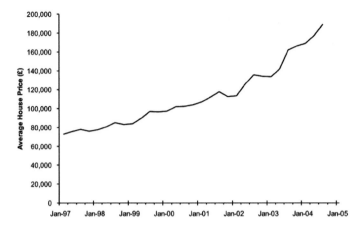

Figures sourced from the Office of the Deputy Prime Minister
Table 504 Housing Market

Fig. 2. Average house price across the UK since 1997.

♦ Choose your property wisely. Select a property which is likely to keep its value and be desirable to buyers in the future.

♦ Choose your area carefully. Know your neighbour-hood well and avoid locations which are likely to change for the worse in the future.

♦ Pay for insurance. Insure against loss or damage to the property.

♦ Take advice. Get a professional second opinion.

Understanding income profit

By letting your property you will receive rental income from which you must deduct expenses, including taxation, to assess your income profit figure. The **yield** of a property is the ratio of the income profit against the capital value of your property given as a percentage figure.

♦ Income profit = rental income – expenses – tax.

♦ Yield = (income profit ÷ capital value of your property) × 100%.

The yield is in many ways very similar to the rates of interest quoted by banks and building societies and will give you a very useful indication of the return you are making on your investment. Some types of property give greater yields than others, often the very cheap end of the market and the very expensive end producing the biggest yield figures.

Maximising your rental income, minimising your risk

♦ Know your letting market. Follow the local letting market over a period of time. Even consider going as far as visiting some properties to assess what is on offer and at what price.

♦ Conduct a market survey. Make certain there is a market for your let and that it is not likely to dry up.

♦ Choose your property with care. Avoid properties with high repair and running costs.

♦ Insure your income. Select a policy which protects against loss of rental income.

♦ Protect your property with an appropriate **lease**.

♦ Select your tenants with care.

PLANNING YOUR LET

To get you started on the road towards assessing your property's (or prospective property's) letting potential, let's look at some of the basics. By the end of this section, you will have made a first pass at some major decisions aimed at formulating the nature of your let. You will have:

◆ identified your target letting market
◆ chosen between a furnished and unfurnished let
◆ assessed your property (or potential property)
◆ considered the use of a **letting agent**
◆ identified any restrictions.

At this stage, this is only a paper exercise and no definite commitment is being asked of you. As you learn you can always go back and change your mind. Eventually you will have enough confidence in your decisions to proceed.

Identifying your market

In all commercial ventures the first step in assuring success is to define and then verify the market for the product or service. As one of your very first steps, therefore, you will need to identify all those sectors of the letting market you could aim for. Some suggestions are:

◆ single student
◆ group of students
◆ single person
◆ group of single persons
◆ couple
◆ family
◆ family with pet(s)
◆ elderly person
◆ elderly couple
◆ budget accommodation
◆ luxury accommodation.

There may be other markets open to you. Draw up your own list.

Conducting a market survey
Evaluating your market is an important step. Be sure your market exists and that there is sufficient demand for your product. There are a number of ways in which you can make an assessment:

1. Contact other landlords.
2. Get in touch with representatives of your target market sector.
3. Speak to accommodation officers.
4. Approach letting agents.
5. Check out the competition.

Remember, your venture will be doomed to failure from the outset if you do not have a market for your product.

Considering a company let
Another possibility is to consider a **company let**. Rather than letting to an individual, a company can take on the tenancy of a property. Under the terms of such an agreement, the company may then house individuals or a family in the property or be free to sublet, usually to one or more of its employees. In the same way, universities and colleges will sometimes rent property from a private individual to house staff or students.

Advantages
♦ It is usually financially secure.
♦ Long, continuous lets are often available.

- Unproductive gaps between tenants are avoided or minimised.
- The company may agree to perform some maintenance duties.

Disadvantages
- It is usually not suitable for short-term lets.
- Property which is not self-contained is rarely sought.
- Property outside 'top of the range' stands little chance.
- A landlord may have little control over who actually occupies his property.

Considering multi occupancy letting

When several unconnected people or groups of people occupy a property or building, often sharing facilities, the term multi occupancy letting will apply and with it comes compliance with a set of specific rules and regulations involving increased fire safety standards, monitoring of occupants to avoid overcrowding and maintenance of services and communal areas. All multi occupancy lettings have to be registered with the local authority and this usually attracts a fee.

In order to convert a property to multi occupancy letting, planning permission will be required for change of use as well as for any structural changes which may be needed. A landlord will also be liable for the payment of council tax, a cost which he can, of course, pass on to his tenants via the rent.

Choosing between a furnished and unfurnished let

Rented property usually falls into one of two categories,

furnished or unfurnished. In theory, however, there is nothing to stop you offering your property with any degree of furnishing you want.

In choosing between furnished and unfurnished letting, points to consider are:

- The market you are aiming for.
- The increased rental income generated by furnished letting.
- The availability and cost of supplying furnishings.
- The extra work and costs involved in maintaining furnishings.
- The extra legal obligations towards safety when supplying furnishings.
- The increased insurance premium to cover contents.

Assessing your property or potential property
Define the property you have (or may have) at your disposal. Where the property is self-contained this is fairly obvious, but where the property to let is part of a larger unit – a room, a group of rooms or a floor in your own home, perhaps – a precise definition is required. Work out if certain facilities will be shared and how you will organise and charge for this. Consider access arrangements and how you could restrict entry to other areas. You may even have to consider the possibility of renovating your property to make it suitable for your purpose.

Matching your property to your market
It is important to match your property to the market(s) you have available to you. The closer you come to

satisfying the needs of your market, the more successful your let will be.

If you have a mismatch, consider the following options.

1. Change the furnishings. Students require desks and book shelves, for example.

2. Upgrade your property. Install a shower, a new kitchen, double glazing or central heating.

3. Re-organise your property. Change the use of some rooms, perhaps.

4. Subdivide. Split a large property into two or more smaller units. This may provide a higher overall yield. It may also provide twice the work!

5. Sell and re-invest. Use the proceeds from the sale of your property to fund one more suited to your needs. This should be your last resort after having considered all other alternatives. The costs of selling and buying will reduce your capital investment, possibly significantly. There may also be taxation implications to consider.

Estimating downtime

From the information gleaned in your market survey, you should have an idea of the rent you can expect from your property. However, there is another aspect to consider in assessing your total rental income. **Downtime** is the period(s) when your property is not producing income. Listed below are factors which will affect your property's downtime:

- The amount of preparation required to make your property ready for let.
- The strength of your letting market.
- The co-operation of your tenants.
- The length of gaps between tenancies.
- The length of the lease – the longer the lease, the less frequently gaps between tenancies will occur.

Identifying running costs
As a landlord, you will meet with expenses. The costs you are most likely to incur are:

- insurance
- repairs and maintenance
- mortgage or loan payments
- letting agent fees
- other professional fees
- wear and tear to furnishings
- advertising
- taxation
- utility services bills
- council tax
- incidental expenses: travelling to the property, rent collection, telephone calls, stationery and stamps, cleaning materials, etc.

When a property is self-contained, the tenant is usually directly responsible for utility service bills and council tax. When not self-contained, the landlord is normally responsible. These expenses are covered more fully in later sections of this book.

Letting mortgaged property

Mortgaged property can only be let with the mortgage provider's permission. Where a property is to be purchased especially for the purpose of letting, a Buy-to-let mortgage can be sourced through many of the leading building societies. (See Chapter 2).

Where the usage of a mortgaged property is to be changed from owner/occupier to tenanted, the mortgage provider must be consulted and, most likely, there will be charges and/or penalties incurred in making the transition. It would be wise also to consult an independent mortgage adviser to provide unbiased recommendations on your situation.

To reduce **income tax** liability, a landlord can choose to offset some or all of his mortgage interest payments against rent received. However, if he already receives some form of mortgage tax relief, he cannot normally get relief on the same interest twice.

The rent-a-room scheme

The **rent-a-room scheme** offers attractive tax relief on rooms rented within your own home. Chapter 11 gives further information.

Using a letting agent

A letting agent is a person or company engaged to perform, on behalf of a landlord, some or most of his letting duties in return for payment. Before deciding whether to use an agent, ask yourself the following questions:

- Do I live within reasonable travelling time of my property?
- Do I have time to take on the day-to-day workload?
- Do I want to work as a landlord?

If you answer 'no' to any of these questions, you are likely to require the services of an agent.

Considering joint ownership

If there is a joint ownership of the property to be let, you should consider:

How will you share the responsibilities and workload of being landlords?
Does this need to be formalised in writing, perhaps as a business plan or as a working agreement?

How will you share the costs/profits?
Who will pay the costs of repair, maintenance, etc? Who will receive the rental payments? Will you share profits according to percentage share of ownership in the property? Will there be a bias in the share of profits towards the one(s) doing the majority of the landlord duties?

Have you considered all the tax implications?
Have you thought through how each owner's personal tax liability may affect the profit figures?

QUESTIONS AND ANSWERS

I'm considering letting my adjoining granny flat for the first time. There are no other properties like it in the area. How can I decide how much rent to charge?

Contact a letting agent, who will be prepared to make a visit to your flat to discuss its potential and give you an idea of the rent you may expect. The letting agent may also be able to answer other general queries. Check if there will be a charge for the visit before deciding to go ahead.

What does it mean when a property is described as self-contained?

It is a term in common use meaning that the property is a whole unit, having its own unshared internal facilities, like bathroom and kitchen. A property sharing outside facilities, such as a drying green or an entrance lobby in a tenement block may still, however, be classified as self-contained.

Is it worth considering letting to students when most will probably opt for student halls of residence?

Certainly, if you can offer a better deal in terms of price or facilities. Some universities and colleges cannot meet demand for accommodation, especially for students after their first year, and there is always a certain percentage of students, especially mature ones, who do not like the idea of staying in halls of residence. Contact the student accommodation officer and get some facts.

FORECASTING YOUR LETTING PROFITABILITY

Now that you have started to think about your own letting situation, this section will help you assess your letting profitability. Attempt a first pass at the figures now, but come back later and refine your calculations as you learn. Consider this an on-going process, improving in accuracy as you gain knowledge and select options.

This basic self-assessment acts only as a guide to likely profitability and in no way substitutes for a professional consultation which is recommended before committing to any path.

Supplying data

To start with, evaluating future income and expenses may seem like trying to look in a crystal ball, as few of the figures will be known with certainty and estimates will have to suffice. But it is worth trying to be as realistic as possible, and some research will be necessary to achieve this. The greater the accuracy you can put into these figures, the more reliable the results.

Forecasting your profit (or loss) figures

Letting should be considered a long term venture and it would be unrealistic to analyse just one year's figures in isolation. In making a profit forecast, look ahead over a few years and you will gain a more accurate overall picture of the profitability of your let.

Use the chart in Figure 3 to calculate your 'net profit after tax' and 'yield' figures, adapting the expenses headings as necessary, to suit your own circumstances.

Analysing your figures

The last two rows of Figure 3, 'net profit after tax' and 'yield', sum up the potential profitability of your let. Remember that yield is a percentage figure, and will give you a measure of the return you may make on your investment.

The capital profit of your property must be taken into account in looking at your investment as a whole. Indeed, you may consider this as being where your primary area of financial gain lies. Whatever your situation, *both* elements of profitability need to be considered in coming to a decision.

In reviewing your proposed investment, make sure your overall financial gain is likely to:

◆ Compare favourably with other forms of investment.
◆ Compensate you for your workload.
◆ Compensate you for the element of risk involved.
◆ Be more than enough to allow for some inaccuracy in your estimates.

TAKING STEPS TOWARDS LETTING

Up to now this has only been a paper exercise. Unless you are very sure of your assessment, it is prudent to consult a professional to look at your letting potential and the analysis you have made before making any binding commitment. A suitable professional may be:

◆ a financial adviser
◆ a solicitor
◆ a bank manager
◆ a letting agent
◆ an accountant.

Income	Year 1	Year 2	Year 3	Year 4	Year 5
Number of months of rental income[1] (a)					
Monthly rent (b)					
Annual rental income (c) = (a) x (b)					
Expenses[2]					
Insurance/council tax					
Repairs and maintenance					
Mortgage/loan payments					
Letting agent fees					
Other professional fees					
Advertising					
Gas/electricity/water					
Stationery/postage					
Use of telephone/car					
Others					
SUB TOTAL					
Add a contingency of, say, 5% for unexpected expenses					
Total expenses (d)					
Profit before tax (e) = (c) − (d)					
Tax (f)					
NET PROFIT AFTER TAX (g) = (e) − (f)					
YIELD[3]					

1 Allow for downtime. 2 These headings may vary according to your situation.
3 Yield is calculated by dividing the net profit after tax (g) by the estimated sum released by the sale of your property after selling costs have been met. Now multiply by 100. Yield is a percentage figure.

$$\text{Yield} = \frac{\text{net profit after tax (g)}}{\text{value of property}} \times 100$$

Fig. 3. An income profit forecast.

There may be a fee for the consultation. Ask in advance how much he or she will charge. You may wish to shop around, but select your adviser carefully and do not choose solely on the basis of cost.

CASE STUDIES

Throughout this book we will follow the progress of two individuals and a couple who turn to letting with different objectives.

Morag wants to earn some extra money

Morag is 30, a housewife with two children aged 5 and 7. Now that both children are at school she has some time on her hands, which she would like to use to earn money for family holidays and extras.

Morag has recently inherited her mother's one-bedroomed flat. She wonders if, instead of finding part-time employment which would present difficulties when the children were off school, she could use her mother's flat and her own spare time to generate an income.

Mike and Ailsa want to let their old house to finance a new home

Mike and Ailsa are a married couple in their thirties with a young family. Mike was made redundant but has found another job in a different part of the country. The family need to relocate but wish to hold on to their old home in case Mike's new job does not work out in the long term. Mike and Ailsa investigate the possibility of renting their old house and using the income to finance a new home.

Stephen wants an investment and to house his student children

Stephen is a businessman and a father of three. His oldest son is in his last year of schooling and intends to go to university which is 30 miles away from home. Stephen has been looking at the costs involved in sending his son to university, mindful that his two younger children may also follow on to further education. Stephen wonders if, by investing in a property suitable for student letting, he may accommodate his student children and also make a tidy profit.

SUMMARY

- Understand what it takes to become a landlord.

- Go over the basics of profit and loss, and consider investment risk.

- Begin your plan to let.

- Assess your potential.

- Check out other types of investment.

- Have your plan checked professionally.

2

Buying to Let

Buy-to-let is a popular form of investment at a time when stockmarket returns have been uncertain. There is currently much speculation on whether the trend of rising house prices will continue and this is certainly a matter for consideration for the potential investor. But, remember, buy-to-let is a long term investment and short-term jitters in the house price statistics should be overlooked in favour of sound long-term projections. Also, rental yield can form a significant portion of the profit and needs to be included in the overall analysis. This chapter looks at selecting a property and financing the purchase, renovating it and applying for grant aid.

CHECKING THE PROPERTY MARKET

If a property is to be purchased, it is sensible to become familiar with the property sales market. There are various ways of achieving this:

- ◆ Read the local newspaper.
- ◆ Obtain copies of local property lists.
- ◆ Speak to estate agents.
- ◆ Tour any preferred neighbourhood.
- ◆ View some properties.
- ◆ Keep abreast with the local economic situation by following the local news.

CHOOSING YOUR BUY-TO-LET MORTGAGE

Most mortgage providers actively promote buy-to-let facilities and recognise it as a sound investment strategy. Competition between mortgage providers means that repayment rates will be keen, matching standard mortgage rates to owner-occupiers. In assessing borrowing limits, projected rental income is allowed as part of the borrower's income calculation and some lenders will consider funding more than one buy-to-let property per borrower.

In determining the viability of a buy-to-let mortgage, it is of course essential to determine whether the rental income will more than cover the mortgage repayments and other expenses. As a general guide, monthly rental income needs to be at least 130% of the monthly loan repayment sum. Unlike standard mortgage schemes, buy-to-let rarely offers '100% of capital' deals, and '85% of capital' is likely to be the maximum on offer.

Mortgage interest payments can be an allowable expense to set against rental income in determining your liability to income tax. Your mortgage provider, local tax office or tax adviser will be able to help you check how this is likely to affect you. Chapter 11 explains more about the effects of taxation on your investment.

A buy-to-let mortgage is sometimes called a Residential Investment Loan and, because they are considered business investments, buy-to-let mortgages are not regulated by The Mortgage Code.

In subscribing to a buy-to-let scheme, you will almost certainly also have to:

- show you have a sound investment plan by providing facts and figures
- agree to a professionally drawn up lease
- use an ARLA registered letting agent to handle the letting
- pay for a comprehensive insurance policy
- agree to certain restrictions on the type of let and/or tenants.

Start organising your finance well ahead of any serious property hunting.

CHOOSING YOUR PROPERTY

Anyone seeking to maximise their capital return should time the buying of their investment very carefully. If the signs are that conditions are not ideal for buying property in your area, consider waiting.

Contacting a conveyancing agent

Nearly everyone will use a professional to conduct the **conveyancing** of their property purchase. If you do not already have a solicitor who handles your business, choose one:

- who comes recommended
- who offers a good, efficient service
- who offers value for money
- you feel comfortable about working with.

Drawing up a list of requirements

To have got this far you will have done a great deal of research and acquired a lot of information about what you require from your property. One way to make sure all that information is brought together usefully is to set down a list of requirements and features to look for in the property you seek. Your list may include the following.

The basic requirement

Type of property, room count, preferred neighbourhood, price limit.

The important features

Type of heating, style of windows, availability of a garden, need for outbuildings or garage, car access arrangements.

Desirable extras

Style of decor, useful accessories such as carpets and curtains, proximity to bus route.

Your list may have alternative or additional entries.

Viewing the property

When viewing a prospective property:

Do
- ◆ remember your market
- ◆ refer to your list of requirements
- ◆ be thorough
- ◆ ask questions
- ◆ be objective
- ◆ view the property in daylight

- take measurements
- arrange a second viewing, if necessary
- have the property professionally surveyed, if seriously interested.

Don't

- view any property outside your price limit
- feel pressured into making a decision until you are ready
- be influenced by fancy decor and furnishings
- compromise on your basic requirements without a serious reassessment of your position.

CASE STUDY

Stephen starts to house-hunt

Stephen and his son spend one afternoon touring round the residential areas close to the university and becoming acquainted with the neighbourhood. They make notes on where shops and the few other commercial premises are located. They also list street names, those which look promising and those to avoid.

Armed with this information, Stephen will be able to make a quick and efficient initial assessment of properties which come on the market and zero in immediately if one crops up in a preferred location.

Experiencing difficulty in finding a property

If you are having difficulty in finding a suitable property, consider the following points.

Your property seeking techniques	
Have you allowed enough time?	New properties come on the market constantly. Be patient.
Are you identifying new properties fast enough?	Get in quickly, ahead of others.
Are you using *all* the sources of supply available to you?	Ask local estate agencies to put you on a mailing list. Check local newspapers and the Internet. Tour areas of interest to catch For Sale signs. Discuss the problem with your solicitor and/or estate agents.
Your plan	
Can you relax any of your less important conditions?	Think carefully of the consequences before doing this.
Are any of your basic requirements unrealistic?	Don't change any of the fundamentals of your plan without a complete reassessment of your situation.

BUYING THE PROPERTY

Be guided by your conveyancing agent when making an offer for the property of your choice. You will probably be in a strong bargaining position because:

♦ your purchase is usually not conditional upon another sale

♦ your finance is ready

♦ you are under no pressure to buy

♦ you can negotiate for extras because they are potentially useful to you

♦ you can probably be flexible about the date of entry.

QUESTIONS AND ANSWERS

When I buy my property, must I allow a sum for stamp duty?

Currently (but subject to change), the stamp duty land tax is: nil up to £120,000, 1% in excess of £120,000, 3% in excess of £250,000, 4% in excess of £500,000. Stamp duty relief for Disadvantaged Areas on properties up to £150,000 may be available. Call the Stamp Tax Helpline on 0845 603 0135 for clarification.

You should also allow a sum for conveyancing fees.

Having never used a building firm before, how can I avoid employing 'cowboys'?

Contact at least two of your prospective builder's recent customers and ask questions like, 'Were you satisfied with the quality of workmanship?' and 'Did the builder keep to scheduled timescales?' and 'Would you employ this builder again?'

A further safeguard is to ensure the builder you choose is a member of a recognised professional body, like the Federation of Master Builders.

I am looking to buy a semi-detached house to let in an area which is mostly owner-occupied. How can I deal with any hostile reaction to my plans from the new neighbours?

There are actions you can take to avoid possible misunderstandings. Introduce yourself to the owners of the houses immediately adjoining your new property and tell them briefly of your plans to let. Explain that the tenants will be selected with care, and that you (or an agent) will be available to discuss any mutual repairs or problems. Any sensible person should respond favourably to such a reasonable approach.

RENOVATING PROPERTY

Renovate = modernise, overhaul, refit, reform, renew, repair, restore.

Renovating property is an avenue that some property investors may wish to explore. The work may range from a fairly minor upgrade through to major structural alterations. Renovation possibilities are:

- *Upgrading and modernising* by installing new windows, heating, door entry systems, etc.

- *Overhauling* by replacing old plumbing, electric wiring, bathrooms and kitchens.

- *Restoring and repairing* walls, roof, disrepair in general.

- *Splitting* one large unit into two or more smaller units.

- *Adapting layout* to something more suitable by changing room usage, sub-dividing rooms, moving internal partitions.

Advantages

- You may require a smaller initial capital outlay.

- You may increase your capital profit and/or your rental income.

- You get the opportunity to form the property to your requirements.

- Grant funding may be available, making it a financially attractive package.

Disadvantages

- It will take time, increasing your property's downtime.
- It will take up a lot of your own time.
- It may increase personal stress levels.
- Mortgage providers may be less inclined to approve where major structural alterations are planned.
- It may increase the level of risk to your investment.

Gathering facts and figures

Deciding to renovate property is a matter for serious consideration. There are a number of methods you can employ in helping to assess the nature and extent of the work to be undertaken, the planning permission requirements and the costs.

Assess the work carefully

Get a professional evaluation of the extent of the work required from an architect/building surveyor.

Estimate the cost

Get a reliable estimate of the cost of the work from an architect/quantity surveyor/building contractor.

Investigate planning permission

Check if planning permission will be required and if it is likely to be granted.

Investigate grant funding
Check if there is grant funding available to offset the costs.

Secure your finance
Check your source of finance for approval.

Take advice
Talk it over with a professional adviser.

Applying for grant aid

Grant aid towards the cost of your renovations may be available via your local authority. Areas most likely to receive grant funding are:

♦ upgrading toilet facilities to an acceptable level

♦ upgrading washing facilities to an acceptable level

♦ installing adequate heating

♦ installing insulation

♦ performing repairs to make the property fit for habitation

♦ performing essential communal repairs where the property is part of a larger building.

Means-testing will apply to the allocation of most grants, and other conditions and restrictions may be imposed depending on central and local government policy at the time. Timing your application to coincide with the availability of funds may also be an important factor to consider.

CASE STUDIES

Morag cuts corners

Morag is sure she will be able to let her property more profitably if she changes her one-bedroomed flat to two by converting her kitchen into a sitting room/kitchen, releasing the lounge to become the second bedroom. This will involve moving an internal partition wall to provide extra space in the kitchen. She knows a DIY enthusiast friend who could do the work.

However, Morag has not investigated the need for planning permission or building warrants. Not only could this venture end up costing much more than she has allowed for, she could find that she has fallen foul of building regulations and land herself in trouble.

Mike and Ailsa fail to get a written quotation

In order to ready their property for letting, Mike and Ailsa employ a local handyman to make some repairs around the house. They have chosen him because he gave a much lower verbal estimate of cost than another tradesman they approached. Mike and Ailsa are upset, therefore, when his final account comes to considerably more than his verbal estimate and they seek legal advice.

Mike and Ailsa discover that had they obtained a firm written quotation, they would have a much stronger case to pursue legally. They have learned too late that it is always best to obtain written details before engaging a workman.

SUMMARY

- Become conversant with the property market.

- Organise your finance.

- Research a mortgage, if required.

- Contact your solicitor regarding conveyancing and for advice.

- Draw up a list of what you want from your property.

- View a selection of properties.

- Ensure you fully understand the extent and cost of any renovation you are considering.

- Check out planning permission requirements.

- Check out grant funding.

- Choose your property with care, keeping your objectives clearly in mind.

- Have the property professionally surveyed and valued before finally committing to the purchase.

3

Organising the Lease

The term lease usually means the contract or written agreement between a landlord and tenant. It sets out terms and conditions, whereby the tenant is allowed to occupy a property owned by the landlord in exchange for financial compensation.

DECIDING TO PUT YOUR TERMS IN WRITING

Setting down the terms and conditions of a let is one of the most important tasks in letting and should be studied carefully.

Looking at what the law has to say about letting

The law has a lot to say about landlords, tenants and their tenancies. It is further complicated by the fact that these laws change from time to time. Keeping up to date, even assuming proficiency in the first place, can be difficult.

The law recognises several types of tenancy and has different names and rules for each. It is vital that you have the right kind of tenancy to suit your situation, and that you know which type of agreement you are entering into and all it entails.

The tenant has many rights in law under any type of tenancy, but it should not be forgotten that so too does the landlord, especially if he commits to a written agreement.

Being aware of Rent Officers and the Rent Assessment Committee

Rent Officers and Rent Assessment Committees are run on a regional basis throughout the UK with local authority support and can be called upon to arbitrate on the amount of rent paid by tenant to landlord. Rent can be set at an amount considered fair in terms of the local market rate.

The Law in Scotland

The law in Scotland regarding new tenancies in the private sector is governed by The Housing (Scotland) Act 1988. Two important types of tenancies are the assured tenancy and the short assured tenancy.

Assured tenancies

One of the main features of this type of agreement is that a referral by the tenant to have the rent set by the Rent Assessment Committee can be avoided. Provided the lease has been drawn up carefully, the landlord can be certain that the rent will remain as agreed.

At the end of the lease, however, it may be possible for the tenant to pursue continued occupancy of the property. Even though, the landlord can still be sure of being granted possession by the courts if any one of a number of mandatory grounds apply, one of which is that the property has been or is intended to be the landlord's home.

Short assured tenancies

This is a distinct type of assured tenancy which gives the landlord extensive powers of repossession over his property provided the proper legal procedures have been followed in setting up and terminating the tenancy.

The tenant, however, has the right to have the rent appraised by the Rent Assessment Committee. It is only likely to change the amount when the rent is considerably out of line with the local market rent.

A short assured tenancy can only apply to lets of duration six months or longer.

The Law in England and Wales

The law in England and Wales regarding new tenancies in the private sector is governed by The Housing Act 1988, amended by The Housing Act 1996. There are two principle types of agreement for new tenancies involving a private landlord; the assured shorthold tenancy and the assured tenancy.

Assured shorthold tenancy

Under this type of agreement the landlord can be certain of obtaining possession of his property at, or soon after, the end of the letting term. There may need to be court action but the landlord does not require to give any qualifying reason for wishing possession of his property.

The tenant, however, may elect to refer the amount of rent to the Rent Assessment Committee who can fix the rent at a lesser sum if they believe that it is considerably out of line with the local market rent.

Assured tenancy

Although most tenancies will be shorthold tenancies, the landlord can choose to offer an ordinary assured tenancy. This type of tenancy offers the landlord less security in terms of regaining vacant possession of his property but it can have other advantages. One of these is that the tenant cannot challenge the amount of rent.

Landlords who have previously lived for some time in their property or are intending to use the property as their home will find that this is safe ground for court action to regain possession of the property.

Being aware of exceptions

It should be noted that company lets, multi occupancy letting and resident landlords all require special consideration and will most likely fall outwith the above tenancy categories.

Understanding the consequences of not having a lease

The consequences of not having a lease are potentially very costly. Some of the results of failing to have a written agreement could be:

◆ Not being able to recover your property to live in.

◆ Having to sell your property with a sitting tenant at a much reduced price.

◆ Having to enter into costly and lengthy court action to resolve differences with the tenant.

◆ Encountering difficulty in increasing the rent.

- Having to accept rent payment in arrears instead of in advance.

- Leaving yourself liable for bills you may consider the tenant's burden.

- Being unable to prevent the tenant using the property in ways you do not want.

- Encountering difficulty with insurance claims because of the tenant's actions.

- Being unable to prevent the tenant subletting.

- Having difficulty in preventing the tenant making alterations to the property.

- Having little control over the keeping of animals on the property.

Drawing up a lease

In sourcing a lease, your main options will be:

- via your letting agent
- via most solicitors (particularly one with a leasing department)
- drawn up by yourself.

The professional preparation of a lease will cost you money (from £50 upwards depending on the supplier and the amount of work required) but ought to be worth every penny in increased personal comfort, knowing that you have properly protected your investment. Shop around for a good deal, but take into consideration the supplier's overall suitability and do not go by cost alone.

CASE STUDIES

Mike and Ailsa notify their agent of an important issue

Mike and Ailsa hope one day to move back to their home when Mike's job allows. When they meet with their letting agent they make sure that the agent understands that it may be important at a future date to be able to regain possession of their house and they discuss realistic timescales when this may happen. In full possession of Mike and Ailsa's expectations, the letting agent is better able to recommend an appropriate type of lease and include the correct detail.

Stephen acquires some background reading

In the course of his work, Stephen is used to consulting professionals to set up business contracts. He knows that it helps to have some basic understanding of the terminology to get the best out of a consultation. Stephen sets himself the task of gathering some background reading on letting so that he will be ready when he comes to discuss matters with his lease provider.

He is content that the cost of the professional lease will be just over 1% of the rental income over the term of the lease.

DRAWING UP YOUR OWN LEASE

If you are certain that you understand the basics of legislation governing letting and your letting circumstances are straightforward and standard, it is possible to draw up the lease yourself. The use of a good quality guide is advised, preferably including specimen leases. The Further Reading section offers recommendations.

(Note that it is inadvisable to draw up your own lease when entering into a company let or when the rent exceeds £25,000 per annum.)

Listing the contents of a lease

The format of a lease may vary but the contents ought to cover:

- a definition of the property and people involved
- a statement of the main terms of the let
- a set of restrictions
- a partitioning of responsibilities
- the terms of penalties and compensation.

Defining the property and people involved

A definition of the property, and those parts to which the tenant has access, will be specified in the documentation. Also recorded will be full particulars of those involved in agreeing the lease, including those of a **guarantor**, if applicable.

Understanding the role of a guarantor

A guarantor is someone who does not reside in the property but guarantees the finance of someone who does. The parent of a student or other young person is the prime example of a guarantor.

Supplying a contact address

There is a legal requirement for a contact address to be supplied to the tenant, to allow him or her to serve legal notices on the landlord.

Stating the main terms of the let

Included in your lease will be statements defining:

- the duration of the agreement
- the rent
- the type of tenancy in law
- the **deposit**
- **inventory** requirements
- the landlord's rights of access to the property
- the tenant's removal from the property.

Defining the duration of the agreement

There are two options in setting the length of your tenancy agreement.

A. *Fixed term agreement.* The lease is for a fixed duration and the end date is specified from the outset. Extensions to the initial term can usually be arranged easily and inexpensively.

B. *Periodic (or free-running) agreement.* The tenancy runs from week to week or month to month and continues until terminated by giving notice. The documentation will state the minimum period of notice required.

Specifying the rent details

Information on the payment of rent will include:

- the amount of rent
- the payment interval
- the due date
- the method of payment

and, possibly

- terms for reviewing (usually, increasing) the rent.

When rent payment is made weekly in a periodic tenancy, the landlord has a legal obligation to provide a rent book for recording payments. It is good business practice, in any case, to issue receipts for monies received from your tenant.

An option to review the rent periodically may be included in the lease if the term of the tenancy is long or if the tenancy is free-running.

Stating the type of tenancy
The legal term for the type of tenancy will be stated, sometimes accompanied by a brief outline of the main features such an agreement means in law.

Setting the deposit
A statement relating to the deposit will cover:

- the amount of the deposit
- what the deposit may be used for
- when the deposit is to be reimbursed.

The amount of the deposit is normally set at a sum equivalent to between four and six weeks' rent. From the landlord's point of view, it is advantageous to set the deposit at an amount greater than that of the final rent payment. This avoids the temptation on the part of the tenant to skip the final rental payment in lieu of a refund in deposit.

It can make the landlord's job easier at the end of a tenancy if a time delay between the end of the tenancy and the payment of the deposit refund, say one month, is specified to allow time to obtain proper costings for any damage or repairs.

Setting inventory requirements
The requirement for an inventory to be verified by signing may be stated in the lease, although the inventory itself is usually furnished separately.

Accessing the property
A lease will assert the landlord's right of access to the property, including emergency access. As well as access rights for repairs and maintenance, consider assuring access to your property for viewing purposes by prospective buyers, follow-on tenants, valuators and surveyors. This will avoid any problems towards the end of a tenancy.

Defining the tenant's removal conditions
A statement covering the conditions of the tenant's removal from the property will appear and may include some legal terms. This will be referred to should the need for eviction arise.

Listing restrictions
A set of restrictions on the use of the property, along with a list of other prohibitions, will be noted in the

documentation. Normally, a landlord of residential property is aiming to restrict usage of his property to avoid business activities. This section of the lease will also give the landlord the opportunity to prohibit specified activities, unless of course he grants permission. In this way the landlord retains the final say on allowing the tenant to make alterations, improvements, etc.

Subletting
It is important to prohibit subletting unless, after discussion with your adviser, there is a real benefit to you in allowing it. If subletting is to be permitted, strict conditional terms ought to be imposed.

Choosing a pets policy
Your policy on whether to allow pets in your property should be well thought out and included as a statement in the lease.

Allocating responsibility
A lease will include a clear indication of the split of responsibilities. Areas covered are likely to include:

- council tax
- water charges
- gas charges
- electricity charges
- telephone charges
- television licence
- insurance cover
- general upkeep, maintenance and repairs.

When the property is self-contained, liability for council tax and utility service bills nearly always falls on the tenant. Where multi-occupancy of a single unit occurs, the landlord often bears these charges and passes on the cost to his tenants through the rent payments.

Assigning responsibility for insurance cover
The landlord usually undertakes to insure the building and contents supplied by him. There may, however, be a clause in the lease preventing the tenant from doing anything which will invalidate the landlord's insurance policy or increase his insurance premiums.

The tenant's own belongings are his or her responsibility to insure.

Stating penalties and compensation rights

Details of penalties borne by the tenant should he or she fail to comply with the terms of the lease will be stated.

CASE STUDY

Morag decides to draft her own lease

When Morag realises she will have to pay over £100 to get a professionally prepared lease, she determines to use her own time and abilities to draw up the lease herself. At the library, Morag is able to borrow two of the books from the Further Reading list, each of which has sections on drawing up leases. In addition, Morag buys (for less than £5) a pro-forma Legal Form covering Short Assured Tenancy Agreements (appropriate for Scotland) from a large stationer in town. Having read the books and having understood the principles involved, Morag uses the pro-forma Lease Agreement she has bought, adding to it a comprehensive list of detailed terms and conditions. She is happy that her completed lease combines both the framework of the basic Lease Agreement and the recommendations of the books.

QUESTIONS AND ANSWERS

I am worried that the lease will be written in such legalistic jargon that I won't know what I am signing. Will this be the case?

No. Leases are mostly very readable and understandable documents. There will be some legal words and phrases, and if these need explaining ask your lease provider for clarification. You will not be asked to sign anything you do not understand.

What happens to a lease after it has been signed?

When a lease has been signed, the master copy is retained by the landlord or his agent, with a copy supplied to each of the other signatories. Stamp Duty Land Tax may be due to the Inland Revenue, payable by the tenant. (See Chapter 7.)

Should I start to arrange the lease before or after I find a suitable tenant?

Definitely before. Consult your lease provider well in advance of advertising for a tenant. With his or her help you will then know the type of tenancy you can offer and the terms such a tenancy implies. Only when you have this information can you consider making contact with a prospective tenant. Any negotiable terms of the tenancy can be put in place at the last minute.

LOOKING AT MULTI OCCUPANCY LETTING

The Housing (Management of Houses in Multiple Occupation) Regulations 1990 defines and governs multi occupancy letting and requires each letting to be registered with the local authority and for that local authority to then monitor the letting, pursuing action should any of the set standards not be met. The Housing Department of the local authority will supply detailed information on the regulations and a registration form. The regulations governing multi occupancy letting include:

- fire safety – fire doors, fire alarms, emergency lighting
- overcrowding
- upkeep of the communal areas
- supply of utility services – electricity, water, gas
- display of statutory notices.

EXPLORING OTHER LEGAL ISSUES

There are a few other legal terms and issues a landlord may come across:

- **resident landlords**
- **squatters**
- eviction
- harassment
- the powers of the Environmental Health Department.

Explaining the term resident landlord
A resident landlord is someone who lives in the same premises as his tenant. Where the law recognises a resident landlord, different rules may apply and, in general, are more likely to favour the landlord.

Coping with squatters
A squatter is someone who gains entry to a vacant property without permission and with the intention of settling there. Squatters have some protection under the law and it will usually require court action to legally evict them.

Pursuing eviction
Under no circumstances does the law permit a landlord to use unreasonable force against a tenant in order to secure an eviction. Usually court action is necessary to secure an eviction and it is always best to fully understand the legal position before taking any steps. (See Chapters 9 and 10.)

Tenants can take court action against a landlord if they believe they have been unlawfully evicted.

Understanding the tenant's right to security and quiet enjoyment
Tenants have the right to enjoy the privacy of their home without harassment or undue disturbance from their landlord. Illegal entry to the property, or use of force against the tenant, would be a matter for the police and may involve criminal charges against the landlord.

Being aware of the Environmental Health Department

A tenant has a right to certain basic living standards, and where these are not met the tenant can complain to the local Environmental Health Department, especially with issues concerning health, hygiene and safety. The Environmental Health Department can take action against the landlord, to enforce repairs for ensuring the provision of a healthy and safe living environment for the tenant.

While repairs are being made on a property, a landlord is required to take adequate account of his tenant's circumstances and may have to provide alternative accommodation.

SUMMARY

◆ Be aware of the consequences of not having a lease.

◆ Decide what you want from your lease.

◆ Know how to obtain a lease.

◆ Aim towards a basic understanding of the law of leases and other legal issues a landlord may come across.

4

Using a Letting Agent

A letting agent is a person or company engaged to perform, on behalf of a landlord, some or most of his letting duties in return for payment. The agent, therefore, can form a buffer between the landlord and tenant, serving as a knowledgeable intermediary, releasing the landlord from some, or most, of his workload. An agent can also offer information and guidance on the majority of letting procedures and be a permanent point of contact for the tenant and landlord.

LOOKING AT LETTING AGENTS

Let's look at different sources of letting agent and the services they can offer.

Finding a letting agent

Letting agents may be found in a variety of different establishments.

Specialised letting agencies

Most areas are served by specialised letting agencies whose only or main business is providing a letting service for property owners. Such agencies usually advertise widely and you should have no trouble identifying those in your area. There are national chains of letting agencies as well as smaller local companies.

Part of a company dealing in property sales

Most estate agencies handle property to let, sometimes alongside their sales and sometimes within a separate section or department. This is an attractive option for those who choose to put their property on the market in the 'to let or for sale' category.

A department in a solicitors' practice

Many large group practices have a leasing department, either separate from or together with their property sales department. This type of agent can often offer most flexibility and will be attractive if your circumstances do not fit the norm.

A solicitor

Some solicitors will take on the role of letting agent, especially if you are already an existing client.

Checking out the services that agents provide

It can vary a lot, but most agents will offer landlords a full, all-encompassing package of services and also a shortened, tenant-finding service.

Defining a full package

Factoring, letting management services, full leasing services, caretaking and other similar terms imply that all or most of the functions of letting are undertaken by the agent. This is likely to include:

◆ evaluating and preparing the property
◆ making safety inspections
◆ advertising
◆ finding a tenant

- checking references
- arranging the lease
- preparing an inventory
- managing the deposit
- collecting rent
- operating a tenant management package
  - making regular inspection visits
  - dealing with complaints
  - pursuing unpaid rent
- operating a property maintenance service
  - arranging routine maintenance
  - organising repairs
- operating an emergency repair service
- conducting an end of tenancy inspection
- providing reports on the property.

With this type of service the tenant pays rent to the agent who in turn reimburses the landlord, less commission and expenses.

Defining a shortened package

A mini package aimed at the front end of a tenancy is often offered under a variety of terms: tenant finding service, tenant and lease arrangement, and others. Exactly what is included in this deal varies but it often covers:

- evaluating the property
- advertising
- finding a tenant
- checking references
- arranging the lease
- receiving the deposit.

Once the tenancy is underway the agent's job is usually over and the remainder of the workload falls on the landlord. With this type of shortened service, rent payments are made directly from tenant to landlord.

Sometimes a rent collecting service is available as an option, for an additional fee.

Seeking other combinations of services
Exactly what you want from a letting agent ought to be a matter of personal choice and there is no harm in seeking out an agent who will satisfy your requirements. Some agents hesitate over deviating from their set packages, and should be avoided if something other than standard is required. If you do opt for a non-standard deal, make sure you have a written agreement clearly defining the split of responsibilities.

ASSESSING CHARGES

Charging structures vary from agent to agent. Most will, however, include some of the following charges:

Full package	Shortened package
A percentage fee for the basic factoring service (usually somewhere between 10 and 20 per cent of the rental income) taken from the rent payments as they are received.	A single lump sum, often based on the rent of the property, e.g. one month's rent.
Single charge for the lease.	Single charge for the lease.
Advertising fees.	Advertising fees.
Single charge for the inventory.	
Property report charges.	

Being aware of other costs

Sometimes other costs may crop up:

- a valuation or assessment charge
- additional advertising charges
- client viewing charges
- fees to organise repairs
- fees to provide written reports
- a safety inspection charge
- costs of pursuing rent arrears
- administration charges.

Further information
- Note that charges are often quoted without VAT (value added tax).
- Certain charges may be split with the tenant.
- Some of these costs will be allowable as tax deductible expenses.

DECIDING WHETHER TO USE AN AGENT

For those who cannot undertake the day-to-day running of their let, the use of an agent will be necessary. However, if the use of a letting agent is optional, consider the following advantages and disadvantages in coming to a decision.

Advantages

- Using an agent makes it easy to get started.
- Using an agent reduces your workload.
- Agents can provide advice and information.
- Agents provide a permanent point of contact for the tenant.
- An emergency repair service may be available.

- It avoids direct contact with the tenant (you may consider this a disadvantage).
- It provides a buffer if there is a grievance with the tenant.
- There may be a legal advisory service.
- Agents may offer you insurance cover tailored to rented property.
- Agencies may offer you a tax advisory service.
- Agents will keep you up to date on legislation changes.
- It may reduce personal worry and stress.

Disadvantages

- Agents' charges can be significant.
- You may have no direct contact with your tenant or property (you may consider this an advantage).
- There is an extra level of administration to negotiate if something goes wrong.
- You are still liable for repair and refurbishment costs, possibly enhanced by an arranging fee.

QUESTIONS AND ANSWERS

I know of no one to recommend a letting agent. How can I check one out?

Apply directly to the agents you are considering and ask them to supply contact names of clients to act as referees. A good agent will have no hesitation in doing this.

Do prospective tenants have to pay to register with an agency?

No. Tenants do not pay registration or introductory fees and will often register with more than one agency.

Who can I contact if I have a complaint about my letting agent?

The Association of Residential Letting Agents (ARLA) is the professional body which governs residential letting agents. Their address is given in the Useful Addresses section.

CHOOSING AN AGENT

In selecting an agent or agency, begin by asking the following questions:

- Are you a member of ARLA (or other recognised professional body)?
- Do you have professional indemnity insurance?
- Do you deal with properties similar to mine?
- Do you cover the area where my property is located?
- What services can you offer?
- What is your charging structure?

Seeking further information

Assuming you are satisfied with the answers to your initial set of questions, ask for more detailed information.

- Do you offer an emergency repair service?
- Can you offer specific legal advice?
- Can you provide safety inspections and certification?
- Do you offer a full repair and/or refurbishment service?
- Can you provide monitoring when the property is not tenanted?
- Can you offer insurance cover?

You may think of other questions to ask.

Making further checks
There are a number of other means open to you in assessing an agent or agency:

- ◆ seek recommendations
- ◆ look at its appeal to potential tenants
- ◆ check on advertising facilities
- ◆ look for helpful and competent staff.

CASE STUDIES

Morag rejects peer pressure
It has never been Morag's intention to use an agent, mainly on grounds of cost. However, one morning she meets for coffee with a group of friends, who tell her quite definitely that *everyone* uses an agent! 'How else will you be able to cope?' they ask rhetorically.

Deflated and full of doubts, Morag spends the afternoon thumbing through the telephone directory and contacting letting agents. Later that evening, however, when the children are asleep, Morag takes time to reassess her situation. Slowly she realises that the use of an agent is *not* essential in her case and her confidence returns.

Mike and Ailsa choose an agency with care
Mike and Ailsa consider the use of an agent essential in their circumstances and feel that it is worth putting some effort into choosing a good one. One afternoon Ailsa

visits all the agencies on their list and assesses each on its merits from the viewpoint of a prospective tenant. Mike and Ailsa will now use this information as an important part of their selection process in determining which agency to choose.

Stephen fails to consider all options

Believing his situation to be unusual, Stephen thinks that the option of using an agent is not available to him. Yet it troubles him that finding time to manage his let in his hectic business schedule will put him under increased stress, a situation his doctor has recently told him to avoid.

What Stephen should have considered was contacting a few agents and his own solicitor, to explain his position and ask what services could be offered to meet his need. It would have only taken a few telephone calls and he may have been able to farm out some of the workload, yet retain the areas he wished to personally oversee.

SUMMARY

- ◆ Decide whether you need a letting agent.

- ◆ Contact ARLA which provides useful information and a list of registered agents in your area.

- ◆ Choose the type of letting service you want.

- ◆ Check out letting agents in your area, seeking recommendations where possible.

- ◆ Understand the charges you are likely to incur.

- Find out whether the letting agent may be able to offer insurance tailored for your let.

- Find out whether the letting agent may be able to offer a tax advisory service.

- Arrange for an agent to visit you and your property.

5

Preparing a Property

Even before you have access to your property, much can be achieved by planning ahead and making advance preparations. Once you do gain entry to your property there are many tasks to be done:

- checking your property's safety
- decorating
- supplying furnishings
- organising the garden, the garage and the outbuildings.

PLANNING AHEAD

Effective planning can save money, effort and time. As well as making lists of work to be done, items to acquire and people to contact, you will have to estimate time-scales. This can be difficult but is necessary in setting the date of the start of your tenancy. This is the date towards which all your planning must aim.

Setting the start date of your tenancy

Factors which will influence the start date of your tenancy are:

- when your property becomes free of the previous occupant

- the amount of preparation required to ready your property for tenancy

- ◆ your own availability

- ◆ the availability of your market (e.g. for students avoid exam time)

- ◆ seasonal events (e.g. Christmas).

Allowing for preparation time

Figure 4 shows the importance of getting the right balance between allowing sufficient time for preparation and starting the tenancy as soon as possible.

Lost time = lost income

A property lying empty of tenants is a property not generating rental income.

Poor preparation = reduced profit

A property not prepared properly may be a property that will be difficult to let or will require increased levels of maintenance in the future.

Good, efficient preparation = minimum loss to downtime/future maintenance

Well planned, carefully executed preparations will achieve all the work necessary to maximise letting potential and minimise future maintenance, in the shortest possible time.

Making advance preparations

There are many ways of making progress even before the property is available to you:

- ◆ Know what work needs to be done.

- ◆ Know what items need to be acquired.

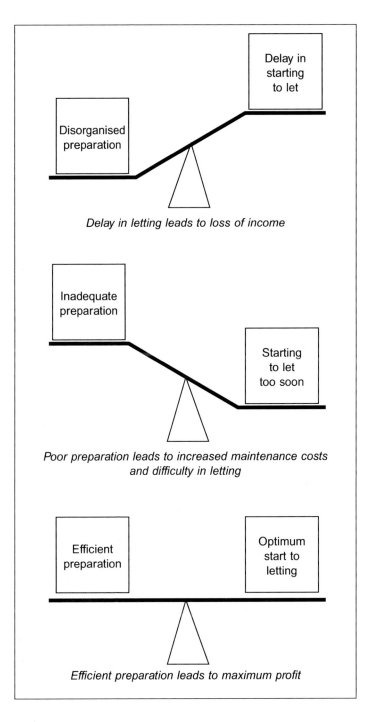

Fig. 4. Balancing preparation time with starting rental income.

- Organise your personal life to make time for preparing your property.

- Arrange for tradesmen to be available if necessary.

- Consider your obligations towards safety.

- Shop around to take advantage of any bargains or special offers.

- Monitor secondhand sources of furniture.

- Gather together the smaller items you need – and the larger items, too, if you have storage.

- Have ready any cleaning or decorating materials you may need.

With these advance preparations made, you are now in a position to be able to make the most efficient use of your property and to minimise its downtime.

CHECKING YOUR PROPERTY'S SAFETY

Landlords have a legal duty to provide a property which is safe to live in. There are hefty penalties for failing to comply. Properties with multiple occupancy accommodation may be subject to extra safety requirements.

Checking the electrics

It is recommended that wiring circuits and sockets be checked at the start of a let and at regular intervals thereafter. As well as the fixed wiring, appliances should be checked for electrical safety and have the correct fuses fitted. If there is any doubt about the electrical safety of any appliance or fixed wiring, you must have it checked professionally.

Checking the gas supply and appliances

The Gas Safety (Installation and Use) Regulations 1998 state that a landlord is responsible for having the gas pipework and appliances certified as being in a safe working condition, that re-inspections are made regularly, at least once per year, and that records are kept of the inspections. Use only tradesmen who are familiar with the Health and Safety Executive requirements and who are registered with the Council for Registered Gas Installers (CORGI).

Using fire detection and prevention devices

Fit smoke detector(s) appropriately, supplied with fresh batteries and maintenance instructions at the start of a tenancy. It is normally expected that the tenant will thereafter have the responsibility for replacing batteries as required.

A small fire extinguisher is an optional extra for the kitchen. Remember that fire extinguishers only have a certain useful lifespan and should be replaced as necessary.

Being aware of fire and furnishings regulations

The law requires that furniture in your property, rented to new tenants after 1 January 1997, complies with the Furniture (Fire Safety) Regulations 1988. Articles covered by the regulations include:

◆ settees
◆ chairs
◆ mattresses
◆ padded headboards

- pillows
- cushions
- loose and stretch furniture covers
- nursery furniture.

All of the above items must carry a government approved label stating compliance with the regulations except mattresses, pillows, cushions and loose furniture covers. Further information on the fire and furnishings regulations can be obtained from:

- your letting agent
- your local trading standards office.

Providing proper operating instructions

Written operating instructions, preferably from the manufacturer, should be provided with each appliance and any potential safety hazard highlighted.

DECORATING YOUR PROPERTY

Your aim is to achieve a decor which is:

- attractive to people from your market sector
- easy and cheap to maintain.

Making it attractive

Attracting a tenant is vital in being successful as a landlord and there is much you can do towards achieving this at little or no extra cost.

- Choose decor which will appeal to your target market.

- Choose light colours for the walls to make the rooms look big and airy.

- Keep it simple and avoid extremes of colour and fashion.

- Provide furniture which is 'flexible' as tenants often wish to change room layouts.

- Do not over-furnish. Tenants need space to add their own belongings.

- Do not supply finishing items, like ornaments, as tenants like to add these themselves.

- Make it look clean and fresh. Cleanliness is a very important consideration for any prospective tenant.

Maintaining the decor

If you intend letting for some time, redecoration costs can mount up. It may be in your long-term best interests to look closely at this aspect now and consider making cost-saving changes from the start.

- Internal walls are usually most easily maintained if they are painted with an emulsion paint.

- Wallpaper can be expensive and is certainly more time-consuming to apply and strip.

- Internal woodwork is often more easily maintained if it is stained or varnished, rather than being gloss painted.

Think carefully about what you can do to make the future maintenance of your property quick and easy.

Making savings

Savings can be made by some simple planning.

1. Choose good quality paints and materials.

2. Choose standard colours from well known brands. These are more likely to be still available in a few years' time.

3. Keep a note of the colour.

4. Use the same colour for more than one room. This will cut down on leftover wastage.

5. Keep leftovers. There may be sufficient to touch up small areas.

6. Use the same colour when you redecorate. Then one coat will probably suffice.

7. Do it yourself, if you have the time and expertise.

Giving guidance to the tenant

The tenant's treatment of your property can have a great effect on the condition of the decor. Issue guidance by advising not to:

◆ stick drawing pins, nails or screws in woodwork
◆ use sellotape or sticky-backed fixings on walls
◆ use nails or inappropriate fixings to hang pictures or mirrors.

A tenant who smokes will cause the decor to require freshening more quickly.

CASE STUDY

Stephen plans his carpeting strategy
Every room of Stephen's flat requires recarpeting. Expecting to keep the property for at least ten years, Stephen decides it is worthwhile investing in a hard-wearing, quality carpet and chooses one which is brightly patterned with a variety of colours. He believes this carpet will be easy to keep and will appeal to the younger age group he will be letting to. Stephen also decides to use the same carpet for every room, thus cutting down on fitting wastage, and he keeps any sizeable cuttings in case a repair may be required in the future.

SUPPLYING FURNISHINGS

In furnishing your property there is one very important point to remember:

What you provide, you have to maintain.

For a fully furnished property a landlord will usually consider supplying items in the following categories.

Will supply
- seating
- tables and chairs
- heating
- beds
- pillows
- bedroom storage furniture
- cooker

- fridge
- washing machine
- kettle
- vacuum cleaner
- full set of crockery
- full set of cutlery
- set of glasses
- full set of pans
- full set of cooking utensils
- iron and ironing board
- curtains/blinds
- gardening tools.

Won't supply
- TV and video recorder
- music/radio equipment
- ornaments
- bed linen
- towels
- specialised kitchen equipment
    - coffee percolator
    - deep fat fryer, etc.

May supply
- blankets, quilts
- dishwasher
- tumble dryer
- microwave oven
- freezer
- toaster
- electric blanket(s)
- nursery furniture.

Sourcing your furnishings

Your main sources of supply will be:

- new from a shop or warehouse
- secondhand from a shop, saleroom or private seller
- from your own home.

	Advantages	**Disadvantages**
Buying new	Usually comes with guarantee Bigger choice You get matching items May offer extended repair warranty Usually instantly available Spare parts usually available Advice available from sales person Comes with operating instructions Convenient Delivery available	Expensive
Buying second-hand	Can be good value for money Can afford to buy better quality	Requires effort to track down bargain May have to wait for availability Riskier – often no guarantees May have to be safety inspected Spare parts may be hard to come by May not have wide choice of style May not have wide choice of colour May require own means of removal

Maintaining the furnishings

When purchasing furniture and appliances, bear in mind that you will have to maintain them. Look out for:

- attractive maintenance warranties
- availability of a local service agent
- availability of spare parts
- safety certification
- the opportunity to purchase extra matching items to replace breakages
- quality.

Minimising maintenance costs

Stick to the following guidelines to keep costs to a minimum but never compromise on safety.

- Do not supply more items than necessary.
- Stick to appliances which offer simple, basic facilities.
- Use recognised, quality brand names.
- See if the repair is something you can do yourself (but safety must never be compromised).
- Avoid call-out fees by taking the faulty item to the repairer, where possible.
- Use a repairer who will offer a guarantee on his or her repair work.
- Have spares of smaller items available so you can replace the faulty item, giving you time to have the original repaired at your convenience.
- Consider re-upholstery rather than replacement.
- Consider chair covers or throw-overs to freshen up a chair or settee.
- Check whether deep cleaning may be all that is required to revitalise a tired carpet.

- Check whether a carpet can be re-tufted/repaired rather than replaced.
- Replace only the mattress rather than the whole bed, if appropriate.
- Check whether replacement may be more cost effective than repair.

CASE STUDY

Morag leaves behind a personal item

Simply because it has always been in the flat, Morag leaves a large dresser which had been given to her mother as a wedding present from her grandmother. The dresser has little real worth but has much sentimental value to Morag. Should anything happen to the dresser in the course of the tenancy, Morag's only compensation will be financial and will not amount to much given the age and condition of the unit.

Morag should have removed any item from the flat with anything more than intrinsic value, as this is all that can be allowed for in a standard tenancy agreement.

QUESTIONS AND ANSWERS

We have an electric ice cream maker which we never use, so we thought we may as well leave it in the furnished cottage we are preparing to let. Is this ok?

No, it's not advisable. If the unit fails you will bear the cost of repair or replacement, as it was part of the original deal. It is highly unlikely that the inclusion of the ice cream maker will make your cottage any more attractive to let or generate any extra rental income, and since it leaves you with the liability of maintenance it is best not to include it in your offer.

I have lost the instruction booklet for the washing machine I am supplying to my tenant. The controls are fairly obvious, so should I just let the tenant work it out for herself or must I try writing out instructions?

By far the best option, although it may cost you a small amount of money, is to contact the manufacturer and have them send you their official user guide/instruction manual. If you do not have an address for the manufacturer a local dealer should be able to help you.

Where can I get detailed information about my responsibilities on matters of safety for multi occupation letting?

Full details of the legislation can be obtained from TSO (see Useful Addresses and Useful Web Sites) for a small fee, and sometimes from a large regional library. A letting agent, solicitor or Citizen's Advice Bureau will also be able to advise you.

ORGANISING OUTDOORS
Where appropriate, a landlord will usually supply:

- a dustbin
- a washing line or rotary clothes drier
- gardening tools.

A set of basic tools in good working order should be supplied if the tenant is to maintain the garden. Compliance with safety regulations is, of course, mandatory if supplying powered gardening equipment.

Minimising maintenance
Easy maintenance is your objective. It may be worth spending time and money at the start of a let in order to create an easily maintained and trouble-free exterior.

Maintaining the buildings
Consider having:

♦ maintenance-free windows
♦ long-lasting exterior coatings applied to walls
♦ maintenance-free eaves and fascia boards
♦ long-lasting weatherproof paint or varnish.

Because they are subject to the elements, any neglected external repairs are likely to have serious and costly consequences. Remember the old proverb: a stitch in time saves nine!

Maintaining the garden and perimeter
Avoid having:

♦ to maintain too many outbuildings
♦ fast growing hedging, trees and shrubs
♦ fencing or railings which require regular painting
♦ large areas requiring weeding
♦ ponds and water pumps
♦ a greenhouse
♦ garden furniture
♦ children's play items.

Consider having:

- minimal or no cultivated area
- slabbed paths and patios
- grass instead of high maintenance garden plots
- stone chips, slabbing or other low maintenance ground coverings
- a tarred driveway.

CASE STUDY

Mike and Ailsa don't recognise a safety hazard
When the children were young Mike built them a climbing frame at the bottom of the garden from some untreated timber. As the children grew older the climbing frame stopped being used and fell into disrepair.

When Mike and Ailsa's letting agent visits to assess the property, she recommends removal of the climbing frame in case the rotting wood gives way and causes an accident.

SUMMARY

- Understand your obligations towards safety and ensure your property and contents comply.

- Decorate your property, keeping in mind
  - its appeal to your market
  - its maintenance.

◆ Supply furnishings, always remembering that what you supply you have to maintain.

◆ Prepare outdoors, keeping the need for maintenance to a minimum.

6

Organising Ahead

The start of your tenancy is drawing near. Consideration now needs to be given to other aspects of your business:

- insurance
- banking arrangements
- paperwork
- recording your property's particulars
- your personal safety.

INSURING YOUR PROPERTY

Paying for insurance cover is a good way to protect your property and reduce the risk to your investment.

Sourcing an insurance policy

Your property will probably be classed as commercial rather than domestic by insurance companies, as you are renting it out. This means that many sources you will be familiar with through advertisements, and from your own home insurance policies, will not be available to you on this occasion. Most of the direct-only companies will not deal with rented property. Many of the remainder impose restrictions on your cover, especially if you want to let to students.

Despite ruling out so many familiar names, there are still insurance sources available to you:

- through your letting agent

- through your mortgage provider

- through the company with which you insure your own home (they may be willing to extend your existing policy)

- through insurance companies who deal in commercial or business cover

- through an insurance broker.

Checking the cover

An insurance policy can provide cover for:

- the building
- the contents
- the rental income
- other liabilities.

Insuring the building

The structure and fabric of your property is insured under this section, providing protection against such events as fire, flood, falling trees, etc.

Insuring the contents

The contents cover should be applied only to the contents *you* supply. It is your tenant's responsibility to supply insurance cover for his or her own belongings. For many insurers this is the section that causes them most concern, as tenants are seen as posing a high risk to contents.

Insuring the rental income

Business interruption, consequential loss and similar

terms are used to mean an insurance cover which will make up lost rental income if damage to the buildings or contents, as defined as allowable in other sections of the policy, prevent you from receiving the full rental income. Your annual rental income is the sum insured in this case.

Insuring against other liabilities

Some policies will offer extra cover, sometimes optional, at an additional cost, and sometimes as part of the standard package. It is worth checking the small print or asking the insurance agent for details. Extra cover may include:

– *Employer's liability.* Only valuable if you employ someone directly.

– *Public liability.* Useful cover against a claim by a member of the public (possibly including your tenant).

– *Legal costs.* Costs of certain legal proceedings may be met but check how relevant this may be to your circumstances. A legal helpline is sometimes offered to provide instant legal advice over the telephone but again check whether queries pertaining to renting and letting can be handled.

– *Personal accident.* Provides cover for you, and possibly any joint owner, in the event of you sustaining injury.

Practical tips

♦ Read the small print or ask your insurance agent to go over the detail.

♦ Watch out for exclusion clauses.

♦ When shopping around, make sure you compare like with like.

♦ Check you are not being asked to pay for cover you don't need.

♦ You may already have sufficient personal accident cover under another policy.

♦ Consider index-linking your policy so that it keeps in line with rising inflation.

♦ Check if there are any discounts available to you.

♦ Check whether the premium you are quoted includes Insurance Premium Tax.

♦ Inform your insurance company of any changes which occur after the start of your policy, as failure to do so may invalidate the cover.

ORGANISING YOUR BANKING ARRANGEMENTS

In the course of your let you will have to both receive and make payments.

Preparing to receive rent payments

When your let starts you will begin to receive regular rent payments. Consider what form you want this payment to take and how you will monitor it.

If you use an agent to collect rent, access to your money may be further delayed by another few days. Your letting agent will normally make payment to you by means of direct bank transfer unless you specifically make other arrangements.

	Advantages	**Disadvantages**
Cash	No processing time or charges	Requires personal collection Security risk
Cheque	Can be posted Reasonably secure	Can bounce Requires you to visit bank Can take several days' clearance time Tenant can forget to send it Small chance of being lost in post
Direct bank transfer into your account	Automatic Easy to check, possibly by phone Secure and traceable	Requires a few days to process

Preparing to meet expenses

The rent payments you receive have to cover expenses and taxes *before* you can begin to think of spending any of it in any other way. Consider:

◆ Setting aside, from every payment received, a sum to go towards meeting your expected tax bill.

◆ Planning ahead for known or predictable expenses.

◆ Setting up a reserve fund to meet unexpected expenses.

◆ Paying your insurance premium by monthly direct debit to spread payment.

CASE STUDIES

Morag organises her banking arrangements

Morag has a joint bank account with her husband. However, she decides she would prefer to keep her property's finances separate and opens a new account in her own name. She chooses an account which allows her to check transactions by telephone as she plans to receive her rental payments by direct bank transfer. Morag also registers to have her interest paid gross, by completing form R85, an Inland Revenue form available from her bank.

QUESTIONS AND ANSWERS

Until last week I have been living in the flat I am about to let and my insurance cover still has six months to run. Will I be better off waiting until it expires before changing it to a commercial policy?

Definitely not. As soon as you let your property you will almost certainly invalidate your original policy, so by allowing it to continue unchanged you will be paying a premium for nothing. See if your current insurers will change or transfer your policy to one suited to your new circumstances. If not, cancel your original policy (with six months still to go, some of your premium will probably be refundable) and set up a new one for rented property.

When should I tell the taxman that I am receiving rental income?

It is best to let your local tax office know of your rental income as soon as you start to receive it. At the end of the tax year, in April, you will then be sent a Land and Property booklet to submit your end of year figures.

If my tenant's rent cheque bounces, my bank will charge me a fee. Can I claim this back from my tenant?

Yes, it is reasonable to expect your tenant to reimburse you for your bank charge in this circumstance. Check the terms of your lease concerning overdue rent payments. You may be entitled to further compensation if payment is late.

COPING WITH PAPERWORK

Paperwork concerning your property and let will accumulate remarkably quickly. Before it gets out of hand or lost, get yourself a filing system. This can take the form of a filing cabinet, a set of document wallets, or even a few cardboard boxes and large envelopes. As long as you feel confident that you can retain and retrieve papers with ease, choose whatever system suits your space availability and your pocket.

Possible headings for your files

- checklists
- correspondence with letting agent
- correspondence with tenant
- correspondence with others
- forms
- insurance
- inventory
- lease details

- operating manuals
- property details – room sizes, paint colour, etc
- receipts for repairs, renewals and maintenance
- receipts for professional services
- receipts for council tax, utility services, insurance
- receipts for other expenditure
- safety regulations and information
- taxation
- useful names, addresses, phone numbers.

Keeping paperwork
The Inland Revenue requires you to keep documentation pertaining to your tax return for at least six years. This is a good rule to apply to all your paperwork.

CASE STUDIES

Mike and Ailsa think ahead

From time to time Mike and Ailsa have had to refer to the operating instructions for their central heating controls, to change settings and functions. Knowing that the tenant will also need to refer to the instructions, Mike prepares to leave the leaflet by the control but feels uneasy about giving up their only copy. As a precaution, Mike decides to photocopy the leaflet, retaining the master for their files. Ailsa agrees that Mike has done well in averting a possible problem in the future.

Stephen gets in a muddle

It surprises Stephen to find how uncontrollable the paper-work for his flat is becoming. His wife is complaining that she can no longer see the coffee table for papers, the dog has chewed some receipts, and Stephen has lost the phone number of a highly recommended painter and decorator he had planned to use.

One evening Stephen spends a couple of hours sorting it all out into a small, portable filing case. He ends up feeling satisfied with his efforts and very much more in control. Stephen grudgingly admits to his wife that he should have done this some time ago.

RECORDING YOUR PROPERTY'S PARTICULARS

Access to your property will be restricted once your tenant moves in. It can be very useful, therefore, to keep a note of your property's particulars for your future ease of reference. Useful information could be:

- ◆ a floor plan of your property
- ◆ room sizes and critical measurements
- ◆ paint colours
- ◆ the source of certain contents so that replacements can be sought
- ◆ the size or type of any consumables, e.g. batteries, filters.

Your memory is *never* as reliable or accurate as a few well-organised notes.

Keeping a photographic record

One of your prime objectives is for your tenants to return

your property and contents to you at the end of their tenancy in the condition in which you supplied them. They should be liable for any discrepancy except for fair wear and tear. Some of the situations when you may expect compensation are when:

- an item is missing
- an item has been replaced without permission
- damage has been done
- the decor has been altered without permission
- structural alterations have been made without permission
- the garden has been altered without permission.

One of the problems in claiming compensation can be in proving the initial condition of the property, furnishings or garden. As most people have access to a camera, an easy and inexpensive solution can be to make a photographic record of your property just prior to letting. Such proof will stand you in good stead, should a claim against your tenants be required during or at the end of their tenancy.

LOOKING AT YOUR PERSONAL SAFETY

As the time to make contact with potential tenants draws near, it is a sad fact of life that you will have to consider your own personal safety. It is very unlikely that any of your applicants will be other than genuine, but it would be foolish to ignore the small possibility that you could be putting yourself at risk. Some simple precautions can and should be taken. The two areas of concern are:

◆ advertising and receiving enquiries about your property

◆ meeting potential tenants at your property.

Advertising and receiving enquiries about your property

There are rules and guidelines for you to follow in placing advertisements and in receiving replies.

Placing an advert

◆ Avoid giving your own address.

◆ Avoid giving the precise address of your property.

◆ Choose a means of first contact carefully: a telephone number, a newspaper box number or *poste restante* address is best.

◆ Avoid giving any personal information about yourself.

Responding to enquiries

◆ Avoid giving your own address.

◆ Avoid giving the full address of your property (unless you are going to invite the applicant to view your property – see below).

◆ Do not respond to telephone enquiries late at night.

◆ Keep your contact businesslike. Do not enter into personal conversation or correspondence.

◆ Avoid giving any personal information about yourself, especially about living alone.

◆ Be aware that it is possible for someone with ulterior motives to have your advertisement details.

Receiving malicious telephone calls

As soon as you advertise your telephone number, you increase your chance of receiving a malicious call. If, as a result of advertising your property, you receive a malicious call:

♦ never give the caller any personal information or your address
♦ do not enter into conversation with the caller
♦ cut off the call by replacing the receiver.

If you are especially concerned by a malicious call or you receive repeated malicious calls, consider:

♦ notifying your telephone company
♦ notifying the police.

Meeting potential tenants

At some point you will have to meet selected applicants at your property. It is a wise precaution to make some check on the applicants' credibility and, more importantly, *never* arrange to meet strangers without being accompanied by a friend or relative.

Checking the applicant's identity

Try to obtain some verifiable detail about your applicants which will help you confirm their identity. You could:

– Ask your caller for their telephone number, then check it tallies by using the 1471 call return service immediately after their call.
– Check the telephone directory to see if the given name, address and telephone number tally.

– Call them at home or work before your meeting – you could confirm your arrangements, perhaps.

– Be alert for any information which does not fit.

– Listen to your inner voice, even if you cannot fully define what is troubling you.

None of these checks is infallible and will not guarantee your safety. Conversely, the failure of any of these checks can have a perfectly innocent explanation and should not necessarily rule out any applicant.

Your best protection is not to meet a stranger alone. Ask a friend to accompany you.

SUMMARY

◆ Insure your property, contents and rental income.

◆ Plan your banking arrangements
  – be ready to receive rent payments
  – decide how you will cope with meeting expenses.

◆ Sort out your paperwork by creating an efficient filing system.

◆ Ensure you are ready to record all monetary transactions in preparation for completing a Tax Return Form.

◆ Inform your local Tax Office that you are going to receive rental income.

◆ Make a record of your property's particulars.

◆ Obtain copies of any instructions or user manuals the tenant may need.

◆ Think carefully about your personal safety.

(7)

Finding a Tenant

Finding the right tenant for your property is an important process. It can be broken down into four distinct stages:

1. Advertising the let.
2. Receiving replies.
3. Viewing the property.
4. Securing the tenancy.

PLANNING YOUR ADVERTISING

Keep your market in mind when planning your advertising and ask yourself:

- What advertising method is most suited to my market?
- Where will my market see my advertisement?
- What wording is most appropriate to my market?
- Is my timing right?
- How can I draw attention to my property?

Selecting a method of advertising

Your means of advertising will depend on your target market and your budget. Some suggestions are:

- word of mouth
- notices in local shop windows
- contacting your local university, colleges, hospitals, large companies

- newspaper advertisements
- via a letting agent.

Can you think of others?

Drawing attention to your property

Look for any feature which makes your property particularly attractive to the category of tenant you have in mind. Some possibilities are:

- students welcome
- pets welcome
- garage available
- parking available
- on a major bus route
- very secluded
- city centre location
- newly refurbished
- large garden
- no garden
- ground floor accommodation
- location – close to hospital/university/large employer/ airport/school.

Your own points can feature in your advertisement and should help to draw the attention of suitable prospective tenants.

Deciding on a budget

Advertising costs can mount alarmingly quickly unless a close check is kept. Establish clearly the total cost of any advertising package you are considering before deciding whether to go ahead. You will often be offered advertising packages in excess of your original enquiry, especially from newspapers. Assess these carefully and, unless sure you are getting a deal you want, stick to your plan and turn them down.

Some free and very cheap methods of advertising, listed above, can be explored first. Bear in mind, however, that paying to advertise widely can sometimes find a tenant more quickly and the extra rent generated may more than offset an advertising fee.

Advertisements – the key headings

Location of property
Give street name or area only. Avoid identifying your property exactly.

Description of property
Keep it brief.

Rent
State the payment interval.

Entry date and length of lease
Add any extra *major* lease details, e.g. guarantor required.

A special feature
Target your intended market.

A means of contact
A telephone contact is the most usual and convenient.

Fig. 5. Key headings for your advertisement.

Wording your advertisement

Advertisements should provide the reader with the basic outline of your offer. Figure 5 provides the key headings which can be used as the basis for your advertisement. Do not include too many details at this stage, whatever your means of advertising. If it is a postcard or poster, get it typed or professionally produced. The quality of your advertisement reflects directly on you and the service you are providing. Aim to create a good impression from the start.

Exact wording will very much depend upon the medium used. Figure 6 shows how to incorporate the key headings into a typical advertisement for a poster, postcard or, possibly, newspaper.

WESTHILL DRIVE AREA
(within walking distance of university)

3 bedroomed flat. Fully furnished

£360 per month

3 or 2 year lease. Entry July

Suit 3 students. Guarantor required

Tel: 01234 567890 between 7 and 9pm.

Fig 6. A sample advertisement incorporating the key headings.

Selecting a means of contact

An advertisement must incorporate instructions on how an interested applicant can contact you. In choosing your method:

- ◆ keep your personal safety in mind (avoid giving your own address)
- ◆ make it easy for the applicant
- ◆ make it convenient for yourself.

Often the simplest means of contact will be by telephone. If you know that you are going to be unavailable for long spells, include times for the caller to expect a reply.

Practical tips

- ◆ Be careful that any contact telephone number is written correctly, especially in passing on details orally.
- ◆ Avoid advertising the exact address of your property. An empty property is always a vulnerable target for burglars and squatters.

USING NEWSPAPER ADVERTISING

Newspapers are, of course, an excellent form of advertising, with the potential to reach a large cross-section of the community at once. There are several points to consider in deciding whether to use newspaper advertising.

Advantages	Disadvantages
Widespread coverage	Expensive
Quick response	Can attract a high percentage of unsuitable replies
	Nuisance callers

Selecting your newspaper

Focus your attention on local newspapers. National newspapers are not suited to advertising single private lets and charge large sums for geographical coverage you do not need.

With your market clearly in mind, investigate which of the local newspapers is likely to reach the largest number of prospective tenants. Daily and weekly papers should be considered equally. Include free-issue local newspapers in your selection procedure.

Choosing the format

Study the advertising format of your selected publication carefully. Normally, there is a choice of:

- box adverts
- line adverts.

Clearly the more space an advert occupies, the more expensive it will be. Figure 7 illustrates examples of box, line and spaced line (line adverts with extra space top and bottom) adverts.

Use the shorthand notation in general usage to cut costs. But be careful not to overdo it otherwise your advert could easily turn into unintelligible gibberish! The newspaper advertising clerk will advise you. Often advertisements are listed alphabetically, so if you consider the position of your advert on the page to be important, choose your first word with care.

Placing the advertisement

Daily newspapers will require a few days' notice to place your advert and weekly publications may need longer. Check this out with a quick enquiry well ahead of your chosen publication date.

To Let

BUNGALOW
5 MILES SOUTH OF CITY

2 dbl.b/rooms. GCH. DG. Decorated to high standard. Garage, garden. Children welcome. No pets. Imm. entry.

£475 p.c.m.

Tel 01221 818181 (d)
01221 242424 (e)

COTTAGE

1 bdrm cottage. Own parking. Small garden. Hilltown Road. £200 pcm + dep. Long lease preferred.
Tel: 01221 909090

Box advert

WEST MONKTON

F/F Semi. 2 bedrms, lounge, bathrm, dining kitchen. GCH. DG. Large garden. Ex. cond. Entry date negotiable. £500 pcm.
To view contact Mrs F Haig on 01221 234567.

ROSELAND. St. ff flat. two dbl. bdrms, din kit, bthrm with shower. CH. Newly dec. Suit students. £235 mthly + dep. Tel 01221 131313.

VINE Street area. 1 bed ff flat. DG. GCH. Private parking. 2 year lease. £325 pcm. Tel 01221 345678.

Line advert with space top and bottom

CITY centre top fl. flat. Part furnished. Sitting rm/kitchen, dbl bdrm, toilet/shwr. Rent £195pcm. Tel. 01221 464646.

GROUND floor flat. FF, Woodville area. 1 large bedroom + living area. 6mths lease only. £150 per mth. Tel. 01221 859855.

ONE Bedroomed flat, near university. £200 pcm + bills. Dep. req. Tel 01221 242424 after 6pm.

TWO Bedroomed terraced house. Walker Ave. Good bus route. Unfurnished. Garage. £195 pcm. Imm. entry. Tel. 01221 454545.

UNFURNISHED 3-bed country house. 10 miles from city. Large fenced-in garden. Pets welcome. £325 pcm. Tel 01333 987654.

Line advert

Fig. 7. Newspaper advertisements: box, spaced line or line.

In a daily publication, often only one particular weekday will feature the majority of 'to let' advertisements, so save your time and money by paying for an advertisement only on that day. You can always readvertise the following week if necessary.

LETTING TO SPECIALISED GROUPS

If your target market is specialised, you are in the fortunate position of being able to focus your advertising and concentrate your efforts. For example, instead of advertising in a general newspaper, it may be advantageous (and cheaper!) to use a specialist journal or magazine.

Letting to students

Student letting can form a significant part of the letting business in those areas close to further education establishments which are liberally dispersed throughout the country, especially within towns and cities. Most universities and colleges operate their own student accommodation office, often employing a full-time student accommodation officer.

Looking at the services of a student accommodation office

The main feature of an accommodation office is the central register of property, which will often be computer based. Adding your details to the student accommodation register is usually free of charge, but it is worth checking this before you go ahead.

The accommodation office may have a noticeboard, for a poster or postcard, and the officer may be willing to distribute handouts of your property details.

Timing your advertising

Timing is very important in targeting the student market. The majority of courses start in the late summer months. Most *new* students will therefore seek accommodation in August and September. However, *current* students seeking to change accommodation may also property-hunt at the end of their exams sessions, which are often in December or January, or in May or June.

Accommodation officers will have a good understanding of their own college's accommodation demand patterns and can be consulted for advice.

Letting to Housing Benefit claimants

Those on low income may apply to the local authority for assistance in meeting the cost of their rent. A tenant's entitlement to housing benefit will depend on a means-tested application to the appropriate section of the Housing Department of the local authority.

The award of housing benefit may meet the rent in full or in part depending on the tenant's financial circumstances and also on the suitability of the property. A tenant's housing needs will be compared to the property's particulars and if these are mismatched, the award may not cover the rent in full. For example, it may be judged that a single person does not require the use of a three bedroomed home, but each case will be considered individually. A rent officer or other Housing Department official may need to view the property as part of the assessment process.

The processing of the claim may take some time and whatever the payment amount, it will always be made in arrears. Payment can be made directly from council to landlord provided the tenant consents.

A landlord should carefully consider the advantages and disadvantages of accepting a housing benefit claimant as a tenant before coming to a decision. Due to the complexity of the regulations and increased level of risk, it is probably best avoided by the inexperienced landlord.

Letting to other specific groups

Other large groups of accommodation seekers may exist in your area. A few suggestions are:

◆ nurses and hospital workers
◆ employees of large local companies
◆ military personnel
◆ entertainment industry personnel.

The personnel department of many large companies will be keen to take details of your property, either for a register or to post on a noticeboard. Many seek short-term accommodation for employees and their families new to the area. Those industries with high mobility staff are a particularly good target, as employees often prefer to rent during their short stay rather than go to the expense of buying a home.

Good local knowledge will help you identify specific groups within your catchment area and understand their needs.

Practical tips

◆ If one particular part of a university, college or large company is especially close to your property, contact the departmental secretary and request notices be posted on the departmental noticeboard.

◆ Universities and colleges often seek accommodation for staff as well as students.

Letting to friends and family

Letting to friends and family needs to be considered carefully and, in general, is not recommended. Your relationship with the tenant *must* be on a business level and you may have to jeopardise your friendship to achieve that. If you do decide to let to a friend or relative, however, you should follow all the same procedures that you would employ for anyone else, such as taking up references, committing to a lease, etc.

DEALING WITH REPLIES

This is your first point of direct contact with your new tenant and it is wise to create a good impression. After all, letting is a two-way process. Whilst you are choosing suitable tenants, they too are choosing a suitable land-lord!

Setting your goals

If all has gone well with marketing and advertising your property, you can expect several or many enquiries. Aim to perform a selection process at this stage. Ideally, you are seeking no more than three or four parties to view the property. You will be wasting your time and that of others by not eliminating those unsuited to your requirements.

Exchanging information

The first contact with an applicant will be a two-way exchange of information.

Landlord → applicant

You must be prepared to give more details of the property, the basic terms of the lease and any other information which may be reasonably required.

Applicant → landlord

In return, you can expect to be provided with details about the applicant, their basic personal circumstances and what they are looking for from a let. Depending on the applicant this information may be freely given, but if not you must ask.

Making preparations for receiving replies

If you are expecting to receive telephone enquiries, choose somewhere quiet to take the calls where you will be without distraction or interruption. A desktop or table nearby, to lay out your paperwork, would be useful.

Preparing appropriate paperwork

To help you deal with your telephone applicants, consider preparing some paperwork.

1. A property checklist. List the main details of your property and lease particulars, as shown in Figure 8. This will serve as a memory aid.

2. A blank information chart. Notes details about your applicants in a chart similar to Figure 9 to help you remember who's who, especially if you receive a lot of

---

CHECKLIST: PROPERTY DETAILS

Accommodation	1 double bedroom	*King size bed*
	1 single bedroom	*Single bed*
	Lounge	
	Kitchen	*Recently refurbished*
	Bathroom	*Shower facility*
	Hallway	*Large storage cupboard*

Facilities   Fully furnished with:
    automatic washing machine
    electric hob and oven
    fridge
    microwave oven
    telephone
    electric storage heating
    double glazing

Rent   £415 per calendar month, payable on 1st of
month
Electricity, telephone, water, council tax are
extra
£500 deposit required

Lease   2 years minimum
Available 1st Sept
No pets
References required

Features   Town centre
Free car parking space
No garden

Fig. 8. A sample checklist of the key features of a property.

calls. Try to get a picture of exactly who will occupy the property and whether their basic requirements match yours.

Inviting the applicants to view the property
Having exchanged information, you should now be in a position to immediately assess the applicant's suitability. This ought to fall neatly into one of three categories:

CHECKLIST: APPLICANT'S FIRST CONTACT DETAILS

Example: Student flat

Contact name_____

Contact tel._____

Who will occupy property?_____

Length of lease?_____

Start of lease?_____

Who will be guarantor?_____

Occupation of property during long holiday spells?_____

Other information volunteered_____

_____

_____

_____

Arrangement made: Arrange viewing ☐ Back-up list ☐

Dismiss ☐

Date/time

Fig. 9. A sample checklist of an applicant's first contact details.

- ◆ suitable
- ◆ unsuitable
- ◆ potentially suitable.

Figure 10 shows how this selection procedure should work.

Dealing with suitable applicants

Invite three or four of those who seem suitable to meet you and view the property. Have a choice of viewing times ready and agree to one which suits your applicant. Try to:

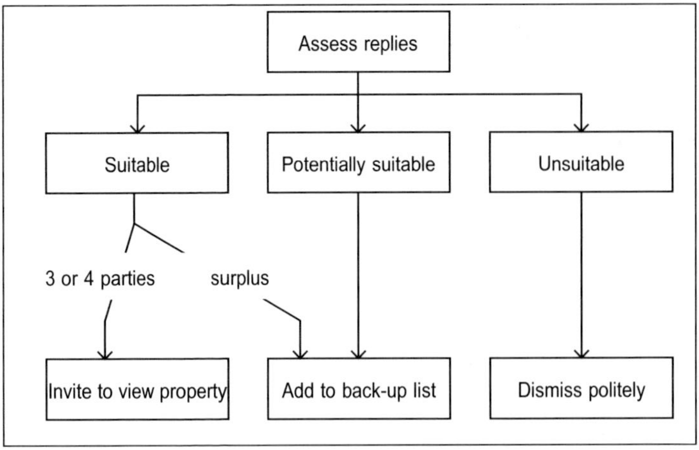

Fig. 10. Dealing with replies.

- arrange *separate* viewing times for each interested party
- see *all* the people involved in a joint application.

Dealing with unsuitable applicants

You will have callers who do not match your needs, and you must tell them so politely. It is only fair to let them know exactly where they stand so they may look elsewhere.

Dealing with potentially suitable applicants

It is possible that you will have callers who may be suitable, except that one aspect of their circumstances would be second choice for you. For example, you may have decided that a three-year lease is your first preference but two years would do. It would be foolish to turn away someone looking for a two-year lease at this stage.

Start a back-up list and keep a note of your applicants' details so that you may contact them later if the property is still available. Treat your surplus callers from your 'suitable' category in the same way and also add them to your back-up list.

VIEWING THE PROPERTY

For some people, preparing to meet prospective tenants can feel nerve-racking. If you feel this way, respond by:

◆ being fully prepared

◆ having all your information to hand

◆ allowing yourself plenty of time

◆ knowing you do not have to make any on-the-spot decisions if you don't want to

◆ having a trial run with a friend cast in the role of applicant.

Preparing a handout

Your applicants may be viewing several properties and a summary of the details of your property will be useful for them to take away as a reminder. A handout would include the main details of the property, as listed in Figure 8, neatly presented. Add your own name and contact details or have a business card available.

Preparing yourself

You, as well as your property, are being assessed by the prospective tenants. Plan ahead and create a good first impression. Ask yourself:

◆ Do I have all the information I need with me?

- Is my paperwork arranged neatly in a folder, so that I can access any part of it easily and quickly?

- Am I dressed appropriately, choosing the sort of clothes I would wear to any other business appointment?

- Do I have plenty of time for the meeting, neither being late nor having to dash away early?

- Can I arrange for the children to be elsewhere?

- If I must take the children, do they have something to quietly occupy themselves while I am busy?

- Have I considered my personal safety?

Preparing the property for viewing

First impressions do matter. A little effort spent now on last minute detail can make a big difference to the image of the property. Consider:

- clearing mail away from the front door
- sweeping leaves from the path
- switching on the main electricity supply
- opening windows if stuffy
- putting on heating if cold
- turning on lights if dark.

Make your own list of pre-viewing tasks.

Ensure you have keys to provide access to all parts of the property and take a torch if necessary.

Conducting a viewing

Points to remember in showing applicants around your property:

1. Suppress a natural tendency to rush.

2. Draw attention to anything which is important, unusual or concealed.

3. Spend a little extra time in the kitchen: there is usually a lot to see there.

4. Point out all the major appliances and state their main features.

5. Open cupboard doors and let the applicants see what is provided.

6. View the outside of the building too: the garden, the parking arrangements, the outbuildings.

Discussing and negotiating

Having toured the property, go over the main points of the lease with your applicants. A checklist is a good idea. If there are questions:

♦ answer them completely and honestly, if you can

♦ do not feel obliged to answer immediately if you are unsure of your reply.

It is at this time that some negotiating may be done. Again, do not feel obliged to reply instantly. Take time to think over any offer or change to the deal you had prepared. If necessary, consult your solicitor or agent for advice.

CASE STUDY

Stephen's preparations minimise time wastage
Being a busy businessman, Stephen's time is a valuable commodity. Yet he considers it important to take the time to personally meet and select the prospective student tenants sharing his flat with his son. Stephen sets out to organise this efficiently.

Having selected four suitable applicants, he arranges individual viewing times of two consecutive appointments on each of two days. He stresses that he wishes notification of any cancellation and also arranges to make a quick phone call to each applicant on the morning of their appointment to double-check they'll attend the meeting. Stephen also asks each student to bring the names of two referees and details of a guarantor.

QUESTIONS AND ANSWERS

Do I have to use a 'special feature' when advertising my let?

No, but it will help tremendously if you do use one. It will make your advertisement stand out from the bunch in the eyes of your target market and increase the percentage of suitable replies you receive.

Often special features go unrecognised. Even the address of a property can be a special feature, promoting its location.

Someone told me I have to serve a notice on my new tenants before I offer them the lease. I'm in Scotland. Is this true?

Yes. In Scotland, if you are to successfully secure a short assured tenancy, form AT5 must be given or sent to your tenants *before* making a binding agreement to let your property. Form AT5 makes it clear that the tenant is being offered a tenancy under Section 32 of the Housing (Scotland) Act 1988. The forms are available from good stationers, letting agents or over the Internet.

Should the offer of a tenancy be made at the end of a viewing, assuming the applicant is suitable?

No definite offer can be made at this stage, because references have to be checked out before a commitment to a lease can be considered. The most you can do at a viewing is to indicate your interest and arrange to take matters further.

Don't be too hasty, in any case. From your point of view, you may have other parties to see. From the applicants' point of view they may wish to discuss the details of this and any other property they have seen between themselves, and may not wish to be rushed.

SECURING THE TENANCY

When you have seen all your applicants you must make a decision on which, if any, of them seem to be best suited as tenants for your property. Do not be afraid to turn them all down and select another batch of three or four from your back-up list if necessary. Even if these too are unsuitable, and there are no alternative interested parties, consider starting afresh by re-advertising rather than accept tenants who do not fulfil your requirements.

Often the steps towards securing the tenancy will be processed by a solicitor or agent, although you can undertake them yourself if you are willing to proceed carefully. These steps are:

1. Checking references.
2. Finalising and signing the lease.
3. Receiving the deposit.

Obtaining references

References should be requested at this stage. At least two references, one character and one financial, should be pursued. A former landlord is, of course, the ideal referee. If a guarantor is involved, you are checking his or her ability to pay so the financial reference should be directed at him or her. You may decide to let your solicitor or agent request the references. There may be a charge for a bank reference.

If you are organising a company let references should still be sought. The company's financial standing should also be checked.

Signing the lease

The finalised lease will require the witnessed signatures of all parties involved:

- the tenant(s)
- the guarantor (if applicable)
- the landlord.

Paying Stamp Duty on leases

Stamp Duty Land Tax (SDLT) replaced the old Stamp Duty on 1 December 2003 and the new SDLT includes paying tax on leases. Normally it is deemed to be the tenant's duty to return the notification (if one is due) to the Inland Revenue and to pay the tax but the landlord has a responsibility to inform his tenants that they should do so. It is an offence not the notify the Inland Revenue if SDLT is due on a lease and there are penalties if the notification is not made within 30 days. All leases of seven years or more must be notified, whether or not tax is due. SDLT rules make no distinction between furnished and unfurnished property.

Calculating whether tax is due

Many residential leases will not attract SDLT. If a quick calculation of

(average annual rent in £) × (length of lease in years)

is less than £120,000, then you need go no further – no SDLT is due.

If this quick calculation yields a figure of £120,000 or more, SDLT may still not be due but a more complex calculation to determine your 'Net Present Value' will be required. The formula for determining your Net Present Value is given in Figure 11 or in Inland Revenue leaflet SD3 or will be calculated for you by telephoning the Stamp Duty Helpline on 0845 603 0135. If the Net Present Value is £120,000 or less, then there is nothing to pay. If it is more than £120,000 then the amount due is 1% of the excess Net Present Value over £120,000.

Properties within a designated Disadvantaged Area have a nil tax threshold of £150,000 instead of £120,000. To find out if your property is within a Disadvantaged Area, telephone the Stamp Duty Helpline or log onto the Inland Revenue website.

(Rent in year 1) ÷ 1.035
   +
(Rent in year 2) ÷ (1.035 × 1.035)
   +
(Rent in year 3) ÷ (1.035 × 1.035 × 1.035)
   +
(Rent in year 4) ÷ (1.035 × 1.035 × 1.035 × 1.035)
   +
(Rent in year 5) ÷ (1.035 × 1.035 × 1.035 × 1.035 × 1.035)
   +
(Rent in year 6) ÷ (1.035 × 1.035 × 1.035 × 1.035 × 1.035 × 1.035)
   +
(Rent in year 7) ÷ (1.035 × 1.035 × 1.035 × 1.035 × 1.035 × 1.035 × 1.035)

   = **Net Present Value** for a lease of up to 7 years

Note: the figure 1.035 is determined by the *Temporal Discount* rate and is subject to change.

Fig. 11. Net Present Value as part of Stamp Duty Land Tax.

Receiving the deposit

As part of securing the tenancy, and as a provision against future damage or rent arrears, tenants should pay a deposit. It is up to you to:

1. Acknowledge receipt.

2. Lodge the payment in a dedicated account opened by you expressly for this purpose.

An account at a bank or building society of your convenience is a good place to lodge the deposit and the sum will accrue some interest over time. This interest will normally be returned to the tenant, along with the capital sum of the deposit at the end of the tenancy less, of course, any deductions which may be necessary.

Informing others

As soon as the tenancy has been secured, inform any other interested parties of your position so that they may look elsewhere. Remember to remove or cancel any remaining advertisements for your property.

CASE STUDY

Mike and Ailsa learn what a deposit is for

It hasn't been easy financially for Mike and Ailsa, as they wait for the rental income from their property to start. They are looking forward to the deposit payment at the start of the tenancy to help them get back on their feet and pay for some extras in their new home. When nothing is received from their agent, Ailsa enquires. She is told that it is agency policy to hold the deposit and the agent reminds Ailsa of the purpose of a deposit and the need to keep it intact.

Mike and Ailsa now understand the difference between rent and deposit and realise that the deposit is not available as disposable income.

COPING WITH DIFFICULTY IN FINDING A TENANT

If you are experiencing difficulty in finding a tenant, review the following areas.

Reviewing the advertising	
Have you allowed enough time for replies?	Advertising through university or company registers can take up to a week for your details to appear and even longer for them to be fully circulated.
Have you tried re-advertising?	Newspaper adverts spaced out by as little as one week can bring a whole new crop of replies.
Try wording the advert differently.	Pick up on another special feature, perhaps.
Advertise more widely.	

Reviewing the package	
Review your rent.	Check your rent is not out of line with the local market rate.
Review your property critically.	Is there some aspect of the property which may be off-putting: does it need decorating? Is the garden a jungle?
Review the terms.	Can you be more flexible? But do not be too hasty to compromise without careful consideration!

Reviewing other options	
Review your market.	Is your advertising reaching your target market? Consider a different market.
Check out the opposition.	Is there a glut of available properties? Are you competitive?
Is your timing right?	Sometimes Christmas and other holidays can be 'flat' times.
Consider using a letting agent.	

CASE STUDY

Morag has difficulty finding a tenant

Morag has aimed her flat at the student market. She has decided to save on advertising costs by using the local college's accommodation register. Three weeks later, at the end of March, she has received only three enquiries, none of which has proved suitable. She decides to contact the personnel department of the local hospital and two large engineering firms. Also, to compensate for her apparent difficulty in attracting a tenant, she places expensive box advertisements in two local newspapers to run for three consecutive days.

Inundated with replies now, Morag has no difficulty in selecting four suitable parties to view her flat and has many more on her back-up list. Pleased to be able to let her flat at last, she regrets her unbalanced and poorly planned advertising strategy. It has not only cost her an unnecessarily large advertising bill, but has also lost her one month's rent through the delay.

SUMMARY

◆ Plan your advertising strategy with your market clearly in mind.

◆ Advertise your let, keeping a close check on costs.

◆ Add your details to college, university or company Accommodation Registers.

◆ Exchange information with applicants.

- Invite three or four applicants to view the property.

- Prepare a handout and, possibly, a business card.

- Make a last minute review of the property to ensure it is at its best for viewing.

- Conduct viewings, avoiding meeting strangers alone.

- Select the most suitable applicant and make a provisional offer.

- Check out references.

- Finalise the lease.

- Receive the deposit.

- Cancel outstanding advertisements and inform others that the property is let.

8

Handing Over the Keys

As the agreed entry date approaches, you are aiming towards:

* making last minute checks
* drawing up an inventory
* meeting the tenant to transfer occupancy.

MAKING FINAL CHECKS

A final check of your property's readiness, confirmation of completion of the lease and receipt of the deposit are all necessary in the run-up to handing over the keys to your property.

Checking your property's readiness

Any last minute repairs or work must be finished. Your tenant has every right to expect all these to be complete unless there has been mutual agreement on any exceptions beforehand. It is in your own interests, too, to have all work finished, as your access to the property when your tenant moves in will be severely restricted.

Checking the lease and payments

Before allowing your tenant access to your property, make certain that:

1. The lease has been signed and is fully complete.

2. The deposit has been received.

3. The first rent payment has been received (unless the rent is payable in arrears).

Consult your solicitor or agent if you have any remaining doubts about giving the keys to your new tenant.

CASE STUDY

Morag has overlooked a defect

Demonstrating the functioning of the door intercom/security system to her new tenant, Morag discovers that it does not work. Although she had checked all the other devices and appliances were working beforehand, she missed out the door entry system because it required two people to check it and whenever she had remembered, she was alone.

Embarrassed to have a breakdown at the very start of the tenancy, Morag promises to have the system repaired as soon as possible. She feels disappointed and annoyed with herself for having made a bad start. If only she had made the effort to check the system was fully functional earlier, she could have saved herself the discomfort of appearing inadequately prepared and the inconvenience of having to make access arrangements with her tenant for repairs.

SUPPLYING AN INVENTORY

The purpose of having an inventory is, at the end of tenancy:

- to highlight missing items
- to identify substitute items
- to identify damage caused by the current tenant
- to identify items which do not belong in the property.

Identifying substitute items

Swapping some of the smaller items of supplied furnishings (curtains, lampshades, pillows, for example) for his or her own, is common practice by many tenants. Most landlords will have no problems with such swaps if their own property is back in place at the end of the tenancy or they choose to accept the alternative offered by the tenant.

It is possible, however, for replacements to be made which are not acceptable. A tenant may substitute an inferior item, either with or without the intention to deceive. If items have been replaced in this way it is necessary for the landlord to be able to identify them and, more importantly, to be able to prove the switch has been made. Possibilities for achieving this are to:

- define each item fully in the inventory, quoting colour, size, model and serial numbers, etc

- code mark all your items using some form of unique, indelible marking

- photograph your property and contents.

Try thinking of other ways of uniquely identifying your contents.

Identifying damage
When damage is identified at the end of a tenancy, it may be difficult to prove whether it was sustained in this tenancy or whether it was there beforehand. In order to avoid this difficulty, all existing damage to items should be recorded at the start of a tenancy. Any further damage, therefore, has to be accepted as being caused by the current tenant. Photographing the contents is a good back-up to recording the condition of furnishings at the start of a tenancy.

Identifying extra items
Unwanted items abandoned by the tenant at the end of the tenancy need to be identified so that the tenant bears the cost of their removal.

Drawing up an inventory
An effective inventory should:

- list all items
- note any existing defects against the item
- quote manufacturer, model and serial numbers
- describe each item fully
- have space to add comments.

To fully list and describe all items can be an onerous, but necessary, task and the inventory can run for many pages. Consider backing up your inventory with photographic records.

TRANSFERRING OCCUPANCY TO THE TENANT

Having worked very hard to get to this stage, the time has come to meet your new tenant at the property to hand over occupancy to him or her. As well as actually handing over the keys, however, you will have to:

- agree the inventory
- read the utility services meters
- go over emergency procedures
- demonstrate the operation of the main appliances and any other systems
- stress key points of importance
- supply courtesy information.

Allow at least one hour for this meeting and make sure your tenant knows in advance it will take this long.

Agreeing the inventory

Your new tenant should be invited to check your prepared inventory and indicate his or her acceptance of the contents by signing. Retain the master copy and furnish the tenant with a copy for their records.

Taking meter readings

If the terms of the lease mean that the tenant has responsibility for gas, electricity or water charges, now is the time to take the meter readings. It is a good idea for both tenant and landlord to retain a note of the readings. It is now your tenant's responsibility to choose a supplier and arrange to be connected.

If you were the previous occupier of the property you are, of course, liable for the payment of these services up to the start of the tenancy and you should settle the accounts directly with the suppliers.

Dealing with the telephone

If your property has a telephone, it is the responsibility of the previous occupier to inform the telephone company that he or she is no longer resident in the property and settle the bill. It is then up to the new tenant to arrange future service. Therefore, unless you were the previous occupier, you need do nothing.

Going over emergency procedures

Consider carefully what action you wish the tenant to take should an emergency or breakdown arise. Your main options will be:

- to call you
- to call a tradesman from a list supplied by you
- to call your agent or some other third party.

Locating emergency turn-off points

Point out the emergency turn-off points for water, gas and electricity. Make sure these are accessible to your tenant and that he or she fully understands what to do.

Pointing out the smoke detectors

Smoke detectors are an effective and inexpensive means of saving lives and ought to be installed in your property. Make sure the detectors are fully operational, with a fresh battery at the start of the tenancy. Provide your tenant with written instructions on the operation and main-tenance of the detector(s).

Issuing operating instructions

The operation of the major appliances should be explained. A quick demonstration may be worthwhile, too, but keep it brief and to the point. Supply operating manuals wherever possible.

Explaining other devices

Your tenant may not be familiar with the operation of some of the other devices you supply, for example:

- ◆ door entry/security intercom
- ◆ central heating controls
- ◆ gardening equipment
- ◆ window security locks.

These should also be explained, and demonstrated too if appropriate.

Passing on other information

You may wish to stress some important points as your tenant takes over care of your property. Some possibilities are:

- ◆ the use of chopping boards to protect the worktops
- ◆ the hanging of mirrors and pictures by using proper wall fixings
- ◆ the need for regular defrosting of the fridge
- ◆ the need to maintain the cooker properly by regular cleaning.

What issues do you consider worth mentioning to your tenant?

Ask yourself if you can help make any of this easier for your tenant by providing chopping boards, coasters, proper wall fixings, etc.

Supplying courtesy information
Although not essential, it is courteous and helpful to supply further information to your new tenant, especially if he or she is new to the area. A few suggestions are:

- refuse collection day
- local bus service details
- local doctor's practice details
- names of immediate neighbours.

Can you think of others?

QUESTIONS AND ANSWERS

My flat is served by a standard BT telephone line. To cut their expenditure, my student tenants don't want telephone facilities. Will I have to pay a fee to disconnect the service? What happens at the end of the tenancy?

Currently there is no fee to disconnect a BT line to a private property. If the line is unused for more than 6 months, the number may be re-assigned and it is possible BT may apply a charge to reconnect if work has to be done to make the line serviceable again.

Do I have to supply the local council with details of my new tenant for their council tax records?

Not usually. If you have previously lived in the property you are now letting, all you need to do is tell the council the date you moved out and where you have moved to. It is the responsibility of the tenant to notify the council of their details.

However, you should always co-operate with supplying information to the council offices if requested to do so as there can be penalties for failing to comply. Remember, if the council believes your property to be empty, the burden of payment falls on you as the owner.

My new tenants want to move in 10 days after the agreed start of their lease. How do I cope with this?

Your new tenants must accept that their responsibility for the property (rent, council tax, utility standing charges, etc) starts on the date agreed on the lease. When they actually move in doesn't really matter.

LOOKING AT KEYS, PRIVACY AND SECURITY

Although ownership of your property will always remain with you, the rights of your tenant need to be considered as your property becomes his or her home.

Issuing keys

A complete set of keys for each adult tenant should be provided. The number of sets should be listed in the inventory and acceptance of this number will therefore be acknowledged by your tenant's signature on the inventory. Include security keys for windows and doors and also keys for all outbuildings to which your tenant has right of access.

Respecting your tenant's right to privacy

If you retain a set of keys, they must be for *emergency use only*. You must:

- *Never* use the keys to gain entry to the property without prior permission unless there is a genuine emergency requiring immediate access.

- *Never* give the keys to anyone else.

- *Always* keep the keys in a secure place.

The law is quite rightly on the side of tenants in terms of protecting the security and privacy of their own home. Any breach of the above rules may mean a landlord is guilty of any one of several possible offences.

Dealing with callers to your property

Agree a policy with your tenant for dealing with callers who have a query regarding your property. Neighbours, officials or tradesmen should be referred to you or your agent to determine a response to their enquiry or proposition. You could:

- allow your name and contact details (or your agent's) to be supplied to such callers

or

- have your tenant take the caller's name and contact details, for you (or your agent) to contact them.

On the same topic, remind your tenant that:

1. You will *always* supply advance notification of any genuine caller such as workmen.

2. They should *never* allow access to your property by anyone unexpected.

Both tenant and landlord have every right to expect such responsible behaviour from each other.

USING CHECKLISTS

There is a lot for everyone to remember at the time of a tenant's entry to your property. Preparing a checklist for yourself is well worth the effort. A handout for your tenant summarising the main points, and especially the emergency and safety issues, may also be worth considering.

Organising the landlord's checklist

Your own checklist may look like this:

♦ issue inventory and get it signed

♦ take electricity meter reading; reading is ....

♦ take gas meter reading; reading is ....

♦ take water meter reading; reading is......................

♦ go over policy regarding emergencies

♦ demonstrate emergency turn-off point – gas

♦ demonstrate emergency turn-off point – electricity

♦ demonstrate emergency turn-off point – water

♦ operation and maintenance of smoke detector

- operation of washing machine – hand over instruction booklet

- operation of hob and oven

- operation of microwave oven – hand over instruction booklet

- operation of central heating controller – hand over instruction booklet

- operation of windows and safety catches

- operation of door entry system

- remind tenant on use of chopping boards to protect worktop surfaces

- go over policy regarding access to property and maintaining security

- go over arrangements for making inspection visits

- give out contact telephone numbers

- pass on courtesy information

- issue keys.

Tick off each item on your checklist as you deal with it at the time of handover.

Organising the tenant's checklist

In a handout to your tenant, consider the following:

- where to locate the emergency turn-off points for gas, electricity and water

- details of approved tradesmen to call in an emergency

- your own contact address and phone number (or that of an agent)

- a reminder of their obligation to provide routine maintenance to certain appliances

- flat inspection arrangements (more on this in Chapter 9)

- a list of courtesy details

- a list of instruction leaflets/manuals provided.

CASE STUDY

Stephen regrets not demonstrating appliances

Stephen does not bother demonstrating the kitchen appliances to his son and his other new student tenants. 'How difficult can it be?' he mutters to himself as he hands over the weighty operating manuals for each machine.

In the following week, a particularly busy spell for Stephen at work, he is interrupted by several telephone calls from his son and flatmates regarding the working of the washing machine. Being remote from the scene, it takes lengthy and complicated discussions over the phone to ensure the operation of the machine has been grasped. Stephen regrets not having taken the time to make sure everything was clear to his tenants when he was there at the flat at the start of the tenancy.

SUMMARY

- Make pre-entry checks:
  - ensure your property is ready
  - confirm the lease is complete
  - check that the deposit has been received.

- Draw up an inventory.

- Meet your tenant and:
  - agree the inventory
  - read the meters
  - go over emergency procedures
  - explain the operation of the appliances
  - pass on courtesy information.

- Respect your tenant's right to privacy.

9

Maintaining the Tenancy

Although the workload of the landlord diminishes when a tenant has settled into his property, there are still routine duties to perform and unscheduled problems to attend to:

♦ monitoring the tenancy
♦ organising repairs
♦ dealing with complaints.

First, though, the developing new relationship between landlord and tenant is worth exploring as failure to adjust can create long-term problems.

RESPONDING TO THE NEW SITUATION

The relationship between landlord and tenant changes enormously when the tenant moves in to a property and makes it his or her home. This can often result in a marked change in attitude from the tenant. A landlord's first visit to his tenant's new home, too, can be unsettling. The tenant has almost certainly marked his or her presence by not only adding personal effects, but also by moving around all the carefully laid out furniture! Sometimes this can create difficulties.

Recognising the symptoms

The tenant may seem:

- unfriendly
- edgy
- brusque
- wary.

Because of this you may feel:

- upset
- annoyed
- worried
- suspicious.

Figure 12 shows how both landlord and tenant can fuel each other's emotions.

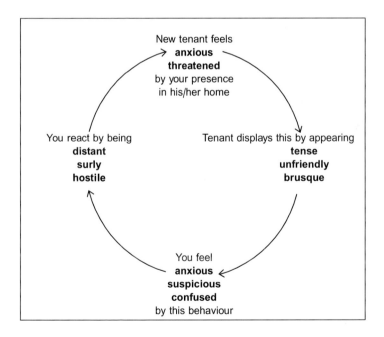

Fig. 12. The vicious circle which can be created by the new tenant/ landlord relationship.

Finding the solution

You must break the vicious circle shown in Figure 12. You can do this by:

- recognising the signs
- adjusting your own expectation levels
- reassuring the tenant your presence is not threatening by the use of suitable behaviour. Adopt a style suited to a visitor in someone else's home.

Can you think of other suggestions to help establish a good working relationship between landlord and tenant?

Coping with the settling-in period

Sometimes there can be a busy settling-in period at the start of a tenancy as the tenant becomes acquainted with his or her new home. They may call on you for help, advice, or with problems and you will have to respond. Match your response to the nature of the query and, to save your time and effort, ask yourself:

- Is this really my problem?
- Can I deal with this by telephone?
- Will meeting the tenant to assess and discuss the problem be easiest in the long run?
- How can I prevent this happening again?

The length of the settling-in period will depend on the tenant and how well you have made your preparations. The odd hiccup will happen with the most thorough of preparations and ought to be accepted as such by both parties.

PROVIDING COMMUNICATION CHANNELS

Adequate channels of communication between you and your tenant are essential for a good working relationship. You are legally obliged to provide your tenant with an address to which correspondence can be sent to you. Often this will be a home address but other options can be:

◆ a business address
◆ a forwarding service
◆ via your solicitor or agent.

Setting up a telephone link

A telephone link can be very useful in speeding up contact between you and your tenant and in dealing with minor issues which do not need to be formally recorded.

Coping with absence

If you find that you are going to be out of contact for some time, and assuming you have no agent, an alternative point of reference for your tenant has to be planned. What arrangements can you make to ensure your tenancy will run smoothly while you are away?

MONITORING THE TENANCY

The routine task of monitoring your tenancy is vital in:

◆ preventing minor problems becoming serious
◆ avoiding expensive court action
◆ showing the tenant you are checking
◆ providing records to back you up.

Checking rent payments

Whatever the method, *always* check the rent payment has

been made as soon as it is due. If payment is by bank transfer it will take three bank working days to process.

Dealing with overdue rent payments
Should a payment be missed, send a written reminder immediately by recorded delivery. Figure 13 shows a sample letter to be sent when a rent payment is first overdue. If there is a guarantor, then this letter should be copied to him/her.

---

40 Lessing Avenue
Oldthorpe OD43 2WE

Tel: (01222) 333444

4th May 200X

Dear Miss Russell,

TENANCY OF 22 UPPER WALK, OLDTHORPE

I have not received your rent payment which was due by cheque on 1st May 200X.

I remind you that payment is overdue and should be made immediately.

I will acknowledge receipt of your rent payment by first class return of post.
Yours sincerely

Dr Christine N Hunter

Fig. 13. A sample letter when rent payment is first overdue.

If this fails to produce payment, then it is worth trying to establish direct contact with your tenant (and guarantor) to gauge the situation. A telephone call or personal visit should be made and remember that this discussion should remain businesslike and you should behave assertively and calmly at all times. Your objectives are:

- to open a communication channel with your tenant (and guarantor)
- to ascertain the facts
- to negotiate a solution.

The details of your lease agreement will state penalties for non-payment of rent but pursuing these through the services of a solicitor or through court action can be stressful and expensive and a negotiated settlement at this point is well worth some effort.

Remember that if a guarantor is involved, it is he or she who is ultimately responsible for the sum overdue plus any charges for late payment.

Keep copies of any letters you send to your tenant (or guarantor) and make written notes of conversations you have with your tenant (or guarantor), ensuring they are dated. If a negotiated settlement is agreed, put this in writing and ask your tenant (and guarantor) to indicate their agreement by signing. Should you decide to take court action in future these written records may be useful.

Pursuing non-payment of rent
If you have failed to extract the rent payment from your tenant (or guarantor) and there seems no hope of a negotiated settlement, then it is time to pursue matters further which probably means court action and/or eviction. Be advised that it is a criminal offence for a landlord to evict a tenant without a court order and you may wish to employ professional help at this stage.

The Law in Scotland regarding rent arrears

The law in Scotland regarding private sector tenancies is governed by The Housing (Scotland) Act 1988. Usually non-payment of rent for a period exceeding three months is sufficient grounds for a Sheriff Court to grant a repossession order whether the lease is an assured tenancy or a short assured tenancy. The court will usually also make an order allowing you to recoup the rent money owed.

Taking the first step

In order to start off the repossession process, you must formally give written notification to your tenant that you want them to leave. It must include:

- your name and address, their name and the property address
- that the reason you are asking them to leave is for rent arrears
- the date you want them to leave by (must be at least 14 days from the date of notification).

Failure to serve this notice correctly may delay the repossession and it is wise to consult a professional to advise you or do this for you. Your sources for advice/assistance are your solicitor, a letting agent or via a specialised landlord service (try *Yellow Pages* or the Internet but choose carefully, seeking recommendations).

Applying for court action

Once the notice has expired and if the tenant has not paid you the rent due or moved out of the property, you may apply for a court order for repossession of your property.

It is highly likely that you will be granted the order if you have followed correct procedure and the Sheriff may also make an award for your court costs to be paid by the tenant. After the court has awarded you the repossession order, you still do not have the right to evict the tenant yourself. Only Sheriff Officers can implement the repossession order.

Avoiding pitfalls

Make sure that you serve written notice correctly and that you follow all the correct procedures. If there are extenuating circumstances, like the property is in poor order, this may weaken your court claim. Also, if the rent arrears is because of a delay in a Housing Benefit claim, the Sheriff is unlikely to grant in your favour; you should have dealt with the Local Authority and the case should not have come to court.

The Law in England and Wales regarding rent arrears

The law in England and Wales regarding private sector tenancies is governed by The Housing Act 1988. If the tenant owes more than two months or eight weeks rent, then the Judge must award you a repossession order.

Taking the first step

In order to start off the repossession process, you must issue a Section 8 Housing Act 1988 notice. This gives the tenant 14 days to respond.

Failure to serve this notice correctly may delay the repossession and it is wise to consult a professional to advise you or do this for you. Your sources for advice/

assistance are your solicitor, a letting agent or via a specialised landlord service (try *Yellow Pages* or the Internet but choose carefully, seeking recommendations).

Applying for court action
Once the Section 8 notice has expired and if the tenant has not paid you the rent due or moved out of your property, you may apply for a hearing at a County Court where the judge must award a repossession order if the rent remains unpaid and in arrears of over two months or eight weeks at the time of the hearing. Exceptions to this will be if the property is in disrepair or if the rent arrears is because of a delay in a Housing Benefit claim in which case you should have dealt with the Local Authority and not have applied to the court.

Implementing the repossession order
Having won the repossession order in court, most tenants will vacate your property as instructed. However, if they do not, you must arrange for Court Bailiffs to remove your tenant.

VISITING THE PROPERTY
The need to visit your property whilst your tenant is resident will occur when:

♦ repairs and maintenance are required
♦ you make inspection visits.

Preparing to visit the property
Except in the rare case of immediate emergency you have no right to enter the property without giving notice to your tenant, at least 24 hours in advance. In practice,

arranging access is usually a case of setting a mutually convenient time by telephone, then following up with written confirmation.

Making regular inspection visits

In order to maintain contact with your tenant and property, regular visits should be arranged. Three months is a common inspection interval, but choose what seems reasonable for your situation. The purpose of the visit is to:

♦ maintain personal contact with your tenant
♦ inspect your property
♦ discuss any problems.

Setting your objectives

In inspecting your property, your main objectives are:

♦ to check for damage, inside and out

♦ to look for anything which requires routine maintenance by you

♦ to monitor anything for which the tenant has the responsibility of maintenance

♦ to be receptive to any indication that the tenancy is not in keeping with the terms of the lease.

Conducting an effective inspection

When organising and making your property inspection, consider the following suggestions.

1. Prepare and use a checklist.

2. Look in every room and outbuilding. It is not reasonable, however, to ask to see in personal storage areas such as wardrobes or drawers unless there is good reason for doing so.

3. Pay particular attention to the kitchen appliances. You should expect them to be in a good, clean condition, with fridge and freezer being defrosted regularly in accordance with the instructions provided. Remember, long-term neglect can result in permanent damage.

Keeping in touch with the neighbourhood

Whilst visiting your property, check round the neighbourhood and make yourself acquainted with any changes taking place in the area. Be especially vigilant if demolition work, building work or road changes are starting, and aim to find out what is happening and how it may affect your property. Your tenant, who is now part of the local community, will be a good source of information about such matters.

Practical tips

◆ Try to arrange an inspection time when there is daylight to inspect the outside of the property.

◆ Catch repairs early: they have a habit of escalating very quickly.

Dealing with an inspection problem

If, after a visit or at any time, there is some aspect of your tenant's care of your property which concerns you:

1. Point it out at once.
2. Follow up in writing.

Aim for agreement with your tenant that the problem will be rectified, then arrange to re-inspect within a short time.

Handling disagreements
If there is disagreement over work that needs doing or over the value of a damaged or broken item, you should arrange for a surveyor or valuer to provide an independent report. Ask the author of the report to include an assessment of how the damage has been caused and this will help you recoup the costs, including the cost of the report, if your tenant is at fault.

If your tenant is liable for costs and the bill exceeds the sum you hold as deposit, you may present your tenant with the account and expect payment. If this is unsuccessful, you can pursue payment through the court system. (See the Further Reading section for information on pursuing court action.)

CASE STUDIES

Mike and Ailsa almost step out of line
On a short holiday Mike and Ailsa find themselves visiting friends and relatives near to their property and, on impulse, are tempted to call on their tenants and check over their old home.

However, at the last moment they realise that this unannounced visit would constitute an impromptu house inspection and would violate accepted procedure, possibly upsetting the balance between tenant, agent and themselves. Instead, Mike and Ailsa settle for a visit to their letting agent and confirm that all is well at their property by discussing the latest inspection report.

Stephen discovers problems during a visit to his flat

When Stephen visits his flat, he discovers damage to the property which has not been reported. A glass panel in an internal door has been broken and all carpets are filthy and requiring vacuuming. It then comes to light that the vacuum cleaner is missing. Stephen asks his tenants to account for the damage and it is agreed after some discussion that the glass breakage was accidental as the tenants moved some furniture, whereas the carpets are dirty because the vacuum cleaner was loaned to a friend and not returned.

Stephen agrees to have the glass professionally replaced and to seek the cost from his insurer with the tenants being responsible for payment of the insurance excess. Stephen gives his tenants one week to have the vacuum cleaner (or an equivalent model) back in the flat and to have the carpets in a reasonable condition. He warns that if this is not done by his next visit, he will replace the vacuum cleaner and have the carpets professionally cleaned both at the tenants' expense.

Stephen puts this in writing to his tenants and keeps a copy for his records.

DEALING WITH REPAIRS

If your tenant reports a fault:

– *Listen.* Try to ascertain exactly what the problem is, in as much detail as possible.

– *Assess.* Decide quickly whether the fault constitutes a safety hazard and, if in any doubt, instruct the tenant to take emergency steps (like turning off the electricity supply). Assess whether you are liable for the repair under the terms of the tenancy.

– *Investigate.* Arrange a visit to inspect the problem for yourself if the fault is unusual or the tenant is vague about the nature of the trouble. The more information you can supply to a repairer, the better and more cost effective the repair service will be.

– *Repair or replace.* Arrange a repair or replacement, if necessary. Remember you will almost certainly need to quote the manufacturer and model number of any faulty appliance to a repairer. You will have this noted on the inventory.

How quickly you respond to a reported fault will depend on circumstances. Certainly, lack of any of the basic services requires immediate attention. Have repairs made professionally to maintain the safety standards of your property and contents. You are required by law to have all gas appliances and pipework properly maintained and to keep a record of work done.

Paying for repairs

The exact terms of who pays for repairs is to be found in the lease documentation. It is normal for the landlord to be responsible for all repairs to the structure of the building and the contents supplied by him, except where the fault or damage has been caused by a deliberate act of the tenant (or by anyone else on the property by the tenant's permission) or by his or her negligence. It is therefore important to establish the cause of the breakage or breakdown, requesting a suitably qualified, independent person to put it in writing, if necessary. If your tenant is liable for the repair, you may present him or her with the bill and expect payment. If this is unsuccessful, you can pursue payment through the court system. (See the Further Reading section for information on taking court action.)

QUESTIONS AND ANSWERS

My tenant has moved out of my property with six months of the lease left and has asked me to re-let. Is this what I should do?

Yes. Even if a tenant leaves without completing the full term of their lease, the landlord is expected to re-let as soon as possible. You can, however, expect your outgoing tenant to continue paying rent until the new tenant takes over payment.

The outside paintwork of my cottage needs attention. Do I still need to notify my tenant even though I do not require entry to the premises?

Yes, your tenant should be informed. Her right of privacy may otherwise be violated by an unexpected painter appearing at her windows!

My tenant always seems to call me with problems late in the evening. Do you think this is reasonable behaviour?

No. Emergency situations aside, you should set reasonable limits on when your tenant may telephone you.

If your tenant is contacting you often, look closely at why and try to remedy the matter(s) once and for all. A tenant ought to be responsible for minor repairs, like changing fuses and light bulbs, and unscheduled contact between tenant and landlord should be infrequent.

DEALING WITH COMPLAINTS

Occasionally you may have to cope with a complaint.

Receiving a complaint from your tenant

If you receive a complaint from your tenant, take the following steps:

1. Stay calm.
2. Acknowledge receipt of the complaint.
3. Gather as much detail as possible about the nature of the grievance.
4. Investigate further and fully assess the situation.
5. Work out your options.
6. Make a decision.
7. Reply to your tenant.
8. Take remedial action, if applicable.

If the complaint is valid aim to put matters right, informing your tenant of your proposals and giving expected timescales. Otherwise, reply that you find no action is required and state your reasons for reaching this decision, backing it up with any available documentation. If you have had to seek advice from a professional, try to have their recommendations available in writing. Figure 14 shows the processes involved in handling a complaint.

Do not ignore complaints. They rarely go away on their own and delay on your part can only weaken your case.

Receiving a complaint from other sources

Complaints about your property
If such complaints come from sources other than your tenant (for example neighbours), you must decide each on its merits how to proceed, employing the basic tactics of Figure 14.

Dealing with complaints about your tenants
In this case, ask yourself whether this has anything to do with you at all. In many cases you would be well advised not to become involved.

If, however, there is a complaint which directly affects your property, your lease or is of a criminal nature, you will need to investigate. Remember, you require proof before you can raise any issue with your tenants or take action through the courts. You may seek the help of the police where you suspect there to be criminal wrong-doing or the Environmental Health Department where it is a matter of public health or safety or noise problems.

Should you choose to pursue eviction, you will need to follow the standard procedures of issuing notification of intent to repossess the property (a Section 8 notice in England and Wales) stating the grounds for doing so, which will be followed by court action to gain the necessary repossession order. See Chapter 10 for more on repossessing your property.

CASE STUDY

Morag deals with a complaint effectively

Morag's tenant has complained that her flat is damp. Morag visits the flat one evening and verifies that condensation forms on the windows and, in the kitchen, gathers in puddles on the window sill. She takes a few days to think matters over, then decides to contact a local building surveyor, and engages him to perform a survey of the property and to provide a brief written report with recommendations. The report states that the building is structurally sound and the problem is condensation. His recommendations are largely aimed at the occupier, and he provides a list of actions geared towards reducing the moisture build-up in the flat. An extractor fan is recommended in the kitchen, which Morag arranges to install.

The written survey satisfies the tenant and Morag has her report for future reference too. Morag feels content that she has dealt with the complaint effectively.

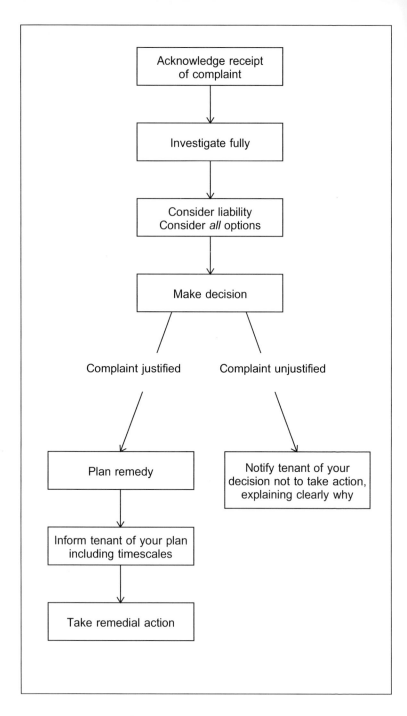

Fig. 14. Dealing with complaints.

SUMMARY

- Adjust to your new role as a landlord.

- Set up an effective communication channel between yourself and the tenant.

- Monitor the tenancy:
  - check rent payments
  - keep receipts and copies of correspondence
  - make regular inspection visits.

- Arrange repairs and routine maintenance.

- Handle complaints effectively.

10

Ending the Tenancy

An increase in workload can be expected by a landlord as a tenancy comes to an end. In addition to dealing with the departing tenant, he has to organise his property's future, whether that be finding a new tenant or selling up.

REVIEWING THE LEGALITIES OF ENDING A TENANCY

How you approach ending your tenancy depends on whether the natural term of the lease has expired or whether you are ending the tenancy early because there is a problem.

The Law in Scotland

The law in Scotland regarding new tenancies in the private sector is governed by The Housing (Scotland) Act 1988. The Scottish Executive issues clear guidelines on serving notice and gaining repossession of privately rented property (see Further Reading section).

Ending the tenancy on or after the date of expiry of the lease – assured tenancy

To gain possession of your property at the agreed end of the tenancy, even though your lease agreement clearly states an end date, you still need to issue your tenants with two months' written notice to quit to satisfy proper legal procedures.

Remember that assured tenancies (in comparison to short assured tenancies) offer less protection to the landlord in terms of regaining the property and court proceedings, where the tenant has done nothing wrong, may not go in favour of the landlord even when the contractual term of the lease has ended.

Ending the tenancy on or after the date of expiry of the lease – short assured tenancy

To gain possession of your property at the agreed end of the tenancy, even though your lease agreement clearly states an end date, you still need to issue your tenants with two months' written notice to quit to satisfy proper legal procedures. The vast majority of tenants will vacate the property on the due date but if not, you may apply for repossession through the Sheriff Court system and be reasonably confident that the ruling will be in your favour. An order granting you repossession should be issued and, again, most remaining tenants will leave your property at this point. But if they do not, your next course of action must be to have the order enforced by Sheriff Officers. Costs for these procedures can usually be recouped from the tenant.

Ending the tenancy before the expiry of the lease

Should you want your property back before the end of the tenancy for personal or business reasons, you can always ask your tenants whether they would be prepared to leave. Some negotiation, possibly with a financial incentive, may be all that is required to reach a satisfactory arrangement. Your tenant, however, does not have to agree to leave during the duration of the lease agreement if the rent is up to date and if they have broken none of the terms and conditions.

If there are grounds for eviction, like rent arrears, criminal activity within the property, anti-social behaviour or breaking one or more of the terms and conditions of the lease, then the written notice to quit need only be of 14 days duration. You will be expected to supply proof of the grounds you state for eviction and the police or the Environmental Health Department may assist you with providing evidence. You will also need to serve notice of your intention to pursue court proceedings to gain possession and finally, if the Sheriff rules in your favour, you will obtain an order for possession from the Sheriff Court. Should your tenant still not vacate your property, you must have the order enforced by Sheriff Officers.

The Law in England and Wales

The law in England and Wales regarding new tenancies in the private sector is governed by The Housing Act 1988, amended by The Housing Act 1996.

Ending the tenancy on or after the date of expiry of the lease

Even though your lease agreement may clearly state the end date of the tenancy, you cannot presume you are entitled to have your property back unless you follow correct procedure in issuing notice to the tenant.

A Section 21 Notice, correctly completed and served at least two months before the date you want your property to be available, will guarantee you have followed proper legal procedures. You do not need to give any reason for wishing repossession of your property. The vast majority of tenants, correctly served with a Section 21 Notice, will vacate the property on the due date but if not, you may apply for repossession through the County Court system and be assured the judge will rule in your favour. An order granting you repossession will be issued and, again, most remaining tenants will leave your property at this point. But if they do not, your next course of action is to have the order enforced by Bailiffs. Costs for these procedures can usually be recouped from the tenant.

Ending the tenancy before the expiry of the lease
Should you want your property back before the end of the tenancy for personal or business reasons, you can always ask your tenants whether they would be prepared to leave. Some negotiation, possibly with a financial incentive, may be all that is required to reach a satisfactory arrangement. Your tenant, however, does not have to agree to leave during the duration of the lease agreement if the rent is up to date and if they have broken none of the terms and conditions.

If you want rid of your tenants because there is a problem, you will be expected to give good cause and to be able to supply proof. Good cause could be for rent arrears, criminal activity within the property, anti-social behaviour or breaking one or more of the terms and conditions of the lease. The police or the Environmental Health Department may assist you with providing evidence.

To start eviction proceedings, a Section 8 Notice, correctly completed and stating the grounds for eviction, needs to be served on your tenants. A Section 8 Notice gives 14 days' notice. This can be followed quickly by County Court proceedings where the judge will consider circumstances and, if the ruling is in your favour, will issue a repossession order. If the tenant still refuses to leave, you can have the order enforced by Bailiffs.

MAKING PREPARATIONS

Your primary aim in renting your property is to make a profit. The changeover of tenants is a time which can significantly influence your profitability. You should consider:

♦ How can I minimise my downtime?

♦ Can I use any gap between tenancies to add value to my property or enhance its letting potential?

♦ Can I use this time of unrestricted access to my property to thoroughly check my property and catch any repairs early?

Scheduling your tasks

Draw up a suitable timetable as the end of your tenancy approaches. It may be similar to the one listed below.

Three months before the tenancy ends
♦ Contact your agent regarding the sending of termination notice or arrange to do it yourself
♦ Consider your property's future.

Within three months of the tenancy ending
♦ Make the last scheduled property inspection.
♦ Plan any repair work.
♦ Plan any upgrading work.

Within four weeks of the tenancy ending
- Start placing adverts to re-let.
- Go through the new tenant selection processes.
- Look for replacement furniture and appliances.
- Organise a cleaning contract, if necessary.
- Contact your tenant to confirm his or her leaving date.

One week before your tenant's expected leaving date
- Contact your outgoing tenant to finalise arrangements.

Making the last scheduled property inspection

Make the most of this opportunity to visit your property and look around specifically from the point of view of noting work which will need to be done after the tenancy ends. Try to ensure you can answer the following questions:

– Does any room require redecoration? Is a full refurbishment required or will a freshen-up be adequate?

– What needs to be repaired? Do I have all the information I need to be able to plan this?

– Is any item coming to the end of its useful life? Do I have all the details I require to be able to organise a replacement in advance?

– Am I likely to have to discuss any damages with my tenant at the end of the tenancy? Do I have sufficient detail to enable me to get an idea of the costs involved?

– How much cleaning is likely to be required? Is soiling excessive? Will I have to make special arrangements or hire specialised cleaning equipment?

Add other queries to your own list.

Upgrading your property

The gap between tenancies is the ideal time to consider upgrading your property or contents. You may consider upgrading if you want to:

♦ increase the value of your investment

♦ rise to a different letting market where the return may be greater

♦ avoid difficulty in re-letting or gain an advantage in re-letting

♦ keep up with the general trend towards improvement in basic living standards.

CASE STUDY

Morag plans ahead and saves money
Now that Morag has accumulated some profit from letting successfully, she plans to use the gap between tenancies to upgrade her flat. From past experience she found that prospective tenants were keen on showering facilities and feels that adding a shower to her bathroom will be an advantage in re-letting.

Well before the tenancy ends, Morag contacts several plumbing and bathroom firms and organises estimates for the work. She makes it quite clear that the work must be carried out and completed within stated dates (the natural gap between tenancies) and insists that the firm of her choice confirms this in writing before accepting their quotation.

The shower installation goes well and Morag is pleased that through her careful planning she got a good price for the job and that the work did not delay re-letting her flat.

PLANNING YOUR APPROACH

Although different landlords may cope with end-of-tenancy arrangements in different ways, one rule which must not be broken is:

> **Never return the deposit until the property has been fully inspected.**

Setting objectives

The key element of the end-of-tenancy process is an inspection of the property. A landlord (or his agent) must make this inspection to determine the level of compensation he may seek from the deposit. In addition to the inspection there are some other duties necessary to terminate a tenancy: these are listed below after the property inspection has been reviewed.

Planning the final inspection

The purpose of a property inspection at the end of a tenancy is:

◆ to check the inventory

- to make sure the tenant has cleared the property of his or her personal belongings, including rubbish
- to check for damage
- to take final meter readings.

Having the tenant present at an end-of-tenancy inspection

The presence of your tenant at an end-of-tenancy inspection is usually recommended. Consider the advantages and disadvantages listed below and ask yourself if you agree.

Advantages

- A tenant may volunteer information about damage or breakages.
- Queries may be cleared up immediately.
- A tenant has the opportunity to rectify a problem (e.g. removing rubbish).
- Meter readings can be taken together, avoiding dispute over accuracy.
- Damage can be discussed there and then, and a course of action agreed.
- Keys can be received and checked.
- A forwarding address can be noted.
- The need for further contact between landlord and outgoing tenant is minimised.

Disadvantages

- Timing the final departure of a tenant can be tricky and could require some flexibility on the part of the landlord.

- A landlord may feel uncomfortable with the presence of a tenant during an inspection.

♦ A landlord may feel pushed into making on-the-spot
  decisions (which he does not have to do!).

CONDUCTING A FINAL INSPECTION

Let's assume your tenant is to be present at the
inspection. (If this is not the case, your inspection
procedure will still be very similar.) Ensure your tenant
knows in advance:

– The inspection will take at least one hour.

– All his or her belongings must be clear of the property.

– He or she is responsible for the removal of rubbish.

– The property and contents must be left in a reasonable
  state of cleanliness.

– He or she will be required to hand over all keys.

– He or she will not have access to the property again.

Checking the inventory

Do not be afraid to take plenty of time over checking the
inventory. Failing to identify a problem now will make it
difficult to claim compensation later. In addition to your
own inspection, ask the tenant if he or she has anything to
report; an honest tenant will give you an honest reply. In
making your inspection, keep in mind the following
points:

Checking all contents are present
♦ Be especially careful to check for smaller, loose items
  like grill trays, fridge shelves, vacuum cleaner attach-
  ments, etc.

- Look upwards, checking lampshades, curtains, blinds and their fittings.

- Don't forget to look in outhouses and check the gardening equipment.

Checking for extra items
- Watch out for abandoned items. Sometimes a tenant will leave a large item of furniture, expecting you to be grateful for the donation. Consider carefully if you really want it; otherwise the cost of removal should be borne by the tenant.

- Do not accept rubbish left in your property. You have a right to expect tenants to remove their rubbish, otherwise you may charge a fee in compensation for having to deal with the disposal of their waste.

Checking the appliances
- Pay particular attention to the kitchen appliances and run through a quick check of their main functions to ensure they are working.

- Check the vacuum cleaner.

- Check any gardening equipment.

- Make sure the fridge and freezer have been completely defrosted, otherwise you may create a flood when you turn off the power.

Checking for damage
- Move furniture, making sure you are thorough.

- Pay particular attention to the carpeting and flooring.

This is an area often overlooked and replacement can be expensive.

♦ Excessive dirt can constitute damage.

♦ All appliances should be in a reasonable state of cleanliness. The cooking appliances are those most at risk and should be examined for damage caused by long-term neglect.

Recovering keys

Make sure you retrieve *all* the keys to your property. A missing set is not acceptable and none of the deposit should be returned until you have all keys in your possession. If all keys are not retrieved, for the security of your property and that of future occupiers, you must change the locks and seek financial compensation from the deposit.

Taking final meter readings

It is the responsibility of the departing tenants to inform the utility companies of their departure and to settle the final bill(s). However, it is sensible to note the final meter readings at the last inspection, getting the tenant to indicate agreement by adding their signature.

Obtaining a forwarding address

It is advisable to obtain a forwarding address for your outgoing tenant.

DEALING WITH THE DEPOSIT

The lease ought to state clearly the terms under which all or part of the deposit is forfeit, but usually you are entitled to withhold:

- The cost of repairs or replacements that do not fall into the category of fair wear and tear.

- The cost of replacing a missing item (including having the locks replaced if keys are not returned).

- A sum to cover unpaid rent or other charges.

- The cost of cleaning, if soiling is beyond normal expectations or caused by the tenant's long-term neglect of routine cleaning and maintenance duties.

- The cost of disposal of rubbish or items abandoned by the tenant.

Informing your tenant

Your tenant has a right to know what sums are being withheld. Give written notification and:

- itemise amounts withheld

- back up your claims with proof of your expenses where possible

- obtain a receipt from your tenant for the amount of deposit you return.

Seeking extra compensation from your tenant

If your costs amount to more than the sum you retain, you may apply to your tenant to pay the excess. Substantiate your claims with proof of your expenses. Should payment not be forthcoming within a reasonable time, consider pursuing settlement through the Small Claims Court, or contact your agent or solicitor for advice.

Avoiding difficulty in dealing with the deposit

Guidelines aimed at minimising deposit problems are listed below.

1. Never return the deposit until your property has been fully inspected.

2. Always keep back an amount you are certain will more than cover your costs until accurate costings are available.

3. Ensure your tenant understands there may be a delay in the return of the deposit while accurate costings are obtained.

4. Obtain real figures and do not guess.

5. Supply your tenant with written copies of costs incurred.

6. Advise your tenant of any lengthy or unexpected delays in obtaining a costing.

7. Obtain written independent valuations or assessments if there is disagreement – the cost of obtaining the report may be split equally between tenant and landlord.

8. Keep your tenant informed.

CASE STUDY

Stephen breaks the rules and loses out

A lamp has been broken by one of Stephen's outgoing student tenants. Stephen has no idea if the lamp can be repaired or if he will have to buy a new one, and he proposes to keep back £50 of the deposit until he can establish exactly the amount involved. While not denying responsibility, the student argues that he was counting on the return of the deposit in full in order to fund a deposit on his new accommodation, and that the deduction will leave him unable to pay and therefore without lodgings. The student asks for a full refund and supplies Stephen with a forwarding address, promising to pay the repair bill promptly. Remembering his own hard-up days as a student, Stephen agrees to a full refund but stresses that he *will* send on the account and expects to be paid in full.

Repair proves impossible and a new lamp costs £34.95. Stephen forwards the account but receives no reply to either his original demand or a reminder. Stephen is now left with the decision as to whether it is worth his time and trouble pursuing the debt. He wishes he had stuck to the rules and retained sufficient funds to cover his costs.

PLANNING YOUR NEXT TENANCY

Approaching the end of one (hopefully, successful!) tenancy, you are probably considering a follow-on tenancy and seeking new tenants. The tenant-finding process can start before your old tenancy ends and run concurrently with your other duties.

Seeking new tenants

All the same sources of supply of tenants are available to you as discussed in Chapter 7, plus one potentially valuable extra source:

◆ your outgoing tenant.

A student will probably know of other students seeking accommodation, a nurse may know of other nurses looking for a flat, etc.

Timing the start of your next tenancy

Timing the start of a follow-on tenancy can be difficult. Clearly, from a financial point of view, the gap between tenancies should be as short as possible. On the other hand, you may need time to:

◆ clean
◆ redecorate
◆ carry out repairs
◆ install replacements
◆ do upgrading work.

The gap you need to leave between tenancies will depend on how much you have to do, how well organised you can be and how co-operative and flexible your outgoing and new tenants are prepared to be. In setting your timescales, try to be realistic. You will often find things take longer than you first thought!

Viewing the property

It is generally expected that an outgoing tenant will co-operate in making the property available for viewing in the last month of their tenancy. Speak to your outgoing tenant about this and arrange a few mutually acceptable time slots for you to offer to your new batch of prospective tenants.

Supplying references

If your outgoing tenant is seeking further rented accommodation, they may ask you for a **reference**. This nearly always requires you to commit to a written reply. In this reply you should aim to confirm:

◆ the identity of the tenant and how long he or she rented your property

and to provide an assessment of:

◆ his or her record of making rent payments
◆ his or her general care of your property
◆ his or her attitude towards your tenancy.

Keep it brief and to the point. Refer to Figure 15 for a sample letter of reference.

Approaching your tenant for a reference
It has always been said that letting is a two-way process. Why not ask your outgoing tenant to supply *you* with a reference as a responsible landlord? Being able to supply confirmation that you are an able landlord must weigh heavily in your favour when you are being considered by prospective tenants.

QUESTIONS AND ANSWERS

My tenant is moving out a few days before his lease is officially at an end. Can I use this time to redecorate, before my new tenant moves in?

It depends on whether your outgoing tenant agrees his tenancy is over. If he does, and hands back the keys to your property, participating in all the end-of-tenancy

18 Castle View
Northbridge BN1 0HH

26th April 200X

Smithwood Property Ltd
Barton
BT65 4MB   Your ref: cl/134/pm

Dear Ms Main,

JANE MARY SIMPSON

I can confirm that Jane Simpson was a tenant in my property in Castle View, Northbridge, for two years from July 200X – July 200X and was jointly responsible with two others for the rent of £390 per month.

Miss Simpson always paid her rent promptly, kept the property in good order and was pleasant and polite in manner. I have no hesitation in recommending Miss Simpson as a suitable tenant.

Yours sincerely,

Marion Davidson (Mrs)

Fig. 15. A sample letter of reference for a former tenant.

procedures ahead of time, there is no reason why you cannot go ahead. If, however, he retains the keys, even though he has removed his belongings and is no longer living there, you may not proceed without his agreement.

Can I sell my flat without an estate agent, using only the minimum necessary legal input?

Yes. You could consider organising the sale of your flat yourself, without incurring the expense of an estate agent.

You may choose to manage the whole process yourself or, perhaps, retain the services of a professional to perform the legal processes of conveyancing. See Further Reading for more information.

Am I liable for payment of the utility services in the gap between tenancies?

Yes. However, where the interval between tenancies is short and there has been little or no use of electricity, gas or water, you may not be billed. If the property is to lie vacant for any length of time, notify the utility services companies in advance. This may save you paying basic or standing charges unnecessarily.

If you do incur utility service charges between tenancies, remember that these costs may be considered as allowable expenses when calculating your tax liability.

SELLING YOUR PROPERTY
Selling property which has been rented can attract a wide range of buyer. Consider other market sectors in addition to the general market. You could sell your property:

♦ as a letting concern to another landlord
♦ fully furnished to a sit-in buyer (assuming your property was furnished before).

The sum raised by selling your property's secondhand furnishings may not amount to much, and to sell fully furnished could be to your overall financial advantage.

Disposing of the contents

A property which looks lived in is often more attractive to a buyer than one with bare walls. While your property is on the market, consider the possibility of leaving most of your furnishings intact.

When the time comes to dispose of the contents, your main options are:

♦ to the property buyer
♦ a house clearance firm
♦ advertising privately in newspapers, shop windows, etc
♦ an auction saleroom
♦ a car boot sale.

Assessing taxation

You will need to carefully assess the effect **capital gains tax** will have on the proceeds of your sale. Ideally this assessment should *precede* your final decision to sell. Refer to Chapter 11 for further information.

CASE STUDY

Mike and Ailsa test the sales market

Mike and Ailsa believe that certain indicators suggest that the property market is now healthier for selling than it has been for some time. Although they have been happy that their old home has adequately financed their new one, Mike and Ailsa decide to test the sales market between tenants. Having deliberately chosen their letting agent as part of a larger estate agency with the possibility of a future sale in mind, they have no difficulty in combining testing the market while maintaining a low-key search for new tenants.

Mike and Ailsa are content that they are covering all angles in their aim to maximise their long-term financial gain.

SUMMARY

◆ Send termination notices.

◆ Forward plan any work to be done when your tenant leaves.

◆ Inspect the property on your tenant's departure.

◆ Read meters.

◆ Refund the deposit.

◆ Seek new tenants, if appropriate.

◆ Prepare to sell, if appropriate.

11

Dealing with Taxation

There are two separate taxes which affect landlords:

◆ income tax
◆ capital gains tax (CGT).

LOOKING AT INCOME TAX

Income Tax is a tax levied on money (or payment in kind) you receive as income after certain allowances have been deducted. The profit you make on rent received from your property is deemed income by the Inland Revenue and is therefore liable to income tax.

Because the rules on what is permitted in allowances are complicated, and further exacerbated by the probability that the rental income is only part of your overall income, individual situations can be very complex and professional advice may be worth seeking. The following section on income tax, as it applies to rental income, gives a basic outline of the fundamental principles. Further reading can provide a more in-depth account.

Clarifying the basic principles

In determining your liability to income tax as a result of receiving rental income, an assessment of your annual profit (or loss) is required. This is done by:

1. Totalling all your rental income for the tax year, including any payments in kind.

2. Subtracting your allowable expenses and certain other allowances.

The resulting profit figure now combines with your income from other sources to assess your overall liability to income tax under the rules in force at the time.

Further information

♦ You must assign your rental income and expenses to the correct tax return period. Tax return periods always run from 6 April of one year through to 5 April of the next. The rental income and expenses you use should be relevant to the period of the return form you are completing.

♦ Rental income is dated according to when it is earned and not to when you actually receive it. This may make a difference to rents due in March or April.

♦ You do not pay income tax on rental profit in isolation from your other sources of income. Your rental profit figure will be combined with your income from other sources, before your overall liability to income tax is calculated, and will include awarding personal allowances appropriate to your individual circumstances.

♦ If you do not have any other source of income, you do not pay income tax unless your rental profit figure exceeds your personal allowances.

♦ A loss can usually be carried forward into future tax years and used to offset a profit.

Looking at allowable expenses

There are many rules on what constitutes an allowable expense. The list below categorises some of the common expenses but it is not comprehensive, nor does it give full qualifying details. Check with your tax office or tax adviser for full particulars of the regulations governing allowable expenses.

Allowable expenses
- rates or council tax
- insurance premiums
- utility service bills
- repairs and maintenance
- renewals
- finance charges (unless claiming Rent-a-room relief)
- lease renewal expenses
- legal fees in seeking advice
- fees in drawing up accounts
- letting agent's fees
- travel to and from the property for any business reason
- stationery
- telephone calls.

Non-allowable expenses
- personal expenses, such as your time
- capital costs
- upgrading costs
- the legal costs of setting up your lease.

Reviewing the 10 per cent wear and tear allowance

If you let on a furnished basis, you may elect to claim this standard allowance. If you do, you can claim 10 per cent of your rental income to cover all your expenses in repairing and replacing the furniture and furnishings. You do not have to give specific details of your expenses if you claim the 10 per cent wear and tear allowance. However, if you elect to claim this allowance, you may not:

- Also claim for specific items which would be covered by the allowance.

- Claim for any excess should you incur wear and tear expenses greater than 10 per cent of your net rental income.

- Change your mind about claiming this allowance from tax year to tax year.

The alternative to claiming this allowance is to claim each wear and tear expense separately as a renewals allowance, backing it up with receipts.

Being aware of the rent-a-room scheme

Special rules can apply if you rent furnished accommodation which is part of your own home. If you qualify, you are entitled to receive up to a certain sum (currently £4,250 per annum, but subject to change) in rent, tax-free.

If the gross income from your rented, furnished accommodation within your own home exceeds the current allowance, you can elect to either:

- pay tax on the excess (expenses are not deductible)

or

◆ opt out of the rent-a-room scheme and pay tax in the normal way.

Careful analysis of your own situation is required before deciding which option is best for you. The decision can be made in hindsight, subject to certain time limits, and it can be changed each tax year to suit your circumstances. Further information can be obtained from Inland Revenue leaflet IR87.

Dealing with joint landlords

Where a 'landlord' is, in fact, more than one person, the Inland Revenue usually assumes your share for tax purposes is the same as your share in ownership of the property. If your situation differs from this, advise the Inland Revenue of a different split.

Looking at landlords who live abroad

Landlords who live abroad and receive rental income from property let in the UK will normally have tax deducted by their letting agent or tenant *before* receiving the rent payment. Exceptions to this will be when:

◆ The rent payment is less than a certain specified amount (currently £100 per week, but subject to change) *and* no letting agent is involved.

◆ The landlord has exemption from the Inland Revenue's Centre for Non Residents (CNR) – formerly The Financial Intermediaries and Claims Office (FICO).

Further information can be found in Inland Revenue leaflet IR140.

Filling in your tax return form

If you need to inform the Inland Revenue of income from rented property, you should acquire the *Land and Property* booklet along with the accompanying notes. Additional helpsheets and leaflets are available from the Inland Revenue on request. There are stiff penalties for the late receipt of tax return forms, so be careful to lodge yours in good time.

Keep all documentation relating to your return form for a minimum of six years after submission. You may be asked to produce some or all of it by the Inland Revenue to back your claims.

Paying income tax

The Inland Revenue will collect any tax payment due in one of two ways:

◆ by sending you a bill
◆ by adjusting your tax code, if you are employed.

Disagreeing with your tax bill

If you disagree with the Inland Revenue's assessment of your tax liability, you may lodge an appeal. Your tax office will tell you how. You have limited time in which to make an appeal, so do it quickly.

LOOKING AT CAPITAL GAINS TAX

In theory, the basic principle of capital gains tax is simple: you are liable to pay tax on any profit you make on the capital or intrinsic value of your property when you sell it or otherwise dispose of it. In practice, however, because of the very many rules, variations, exemptions and allowances which accompany CGT, there is a great deal to consider when looking at your CGT liability and it may be worth consulting a specialist to discuss your individual situation.

The section which follows gives a basic outline of the general principles of CGT and some clarification of terms used by the Inland Revenue. It is not intended to cover the full story: that would take another book!

Clarifying the basic principles

CGT is a tax levied on the profit you make from the capital value of your property when you dispose of it. Usually, this is the difference between the buying and selling prices, less certain allowances which are deductible. This profit (or loss) figure is combined with any other profit (or loss) figures from other disposals you may have made in that tax year and tax is calculated according to the rules in force at the time.

Further information

◆ You do not pay tax on the whole of the proceeds of a sale, only on the *increase* in value of your property whilst you have owned it and after certain allowances have been deducted.

◆ If there is no element of profit, there is no liability to CGT tax.

◆ You have no liability to CGT tax until you dispose of your property, usually by selling.

◆ The date of sale (or disposal) of your property determines which tax year your CGT liability applies to.

- Any profit (or loss) as a result of selling your property must be taken together with the profit or loss from other disposal(s) you have made in that tax year before your liability to CGT can be assessed.

- If losses incurred by you in this or previous years can more than offset any gain you have made, you may have no liability to CGT.

- You have an annual CGT personal allowance and do not pay CGT unless your total disposal profit exceeds this figure. The amount of this allowance is liable to change from time to time, usually at a Budget.

- If you owned the property before March 1982, you can elect to use the market value of the property in March 1982 as your acquisition cost.

- If disposal of your property is by transfer to your husband or wife, assuming you are living together, there is no liability to CGT.

- Your CGT bill may be reduced by one or more allowances or reliefs outlined later in this chapter.

Defining chargeable gain and allowable loss
Chargeable gain is a term used by the Inland Revenue to mean that element of profit you make on the value of your property between acquiring it and disposing of it. Usually, this is the difference between the buying and selling price, less certain allowances which are deductible.

Allowable loss is the term used if you have made a loss instead of a profit.

Looking at expenses

The Inland Revenue recognises the following allowable expenses in assessing liability to CGT:

- acquisition costs
- enhancement costs
- incidental costs of acquisition or disposal
- expenditure on defending or establishing your right over the asset.

Explaining the terms

- Acquisition costs are the amounts you paid to acquire (usually buy) your property.

- If you inherited or were gifted your property, the Inland Revenue assumes the acquisition cost to be the market value of your property on the date of death of the testator or on the date of transfer.

- Enhancement costs are those expenses you have incurred in upgrading, improving or adding value to your property.

- Installing central heating or double glazing, or adding an extension, are examples of what may be acceptable as enhancement costs.

- You cannot claim an enhancement cost if the improvement no longer exists at the time of sale (or disposal) of your property.

- Incidental costs are those expenses incurred by you in acquiring and disposing of (usually buying and selling) your property.

- Incidental costs include:
  - professional fees for a solicitor or building surveyor
  - conveyancing costs
  - advertising costs incurred in seeking a buyer
  - estate agency fees
  - stamp duty.

- If you have had any dispute over your right to your property or any part of it, you may deduct the costs incurred by you in pursuing this, including legal costs.

Reviewing taper relief

Taper Relief, introduced in April 1998, can reduce your liability to capital gains tax. The basic idea is that the longer you own a property, the less CGT you pay. The simple calculation is made by applying a percentage figure from a table supplied by the Inland Revenue to your gain, dependent on the number of whole years you have owned your property after April 1998. The exact percentage figure by which you can reduce your gain is available from Inland Revenue leaflet CGT1. Your local tax office or tax adviser will also be able to advise you.

Reviewing indexation

Indexation, which preceded Taper Relief, was a special allowance geared to compensate you for the general trend of inflationary price rises. The Finance Act 1998 froze this allowance at April 1998 and an indexation allowance will therefore not be available to you unless you owned your property before that date. This allowance is set by applying a simple calculation to your gain, using numbers obtained from government issued Retail Price Index (RPI) figures.

When due, an indexation allowance:

◆ will reduce your chargeable gain and the tax you pay on it
◆ will not be applied if you made a loss instead of a profit from the sale of your property
◆ may only reduce your chargeable gain to a minimum of zero: it cannot be used to turn a profit into a loss.

Your regional library keeps lists of RPI figures in a publication called *Monthly Digest of Statistics*, issued by the Office for National Statistics.

If the dates of ownership of your property mean that you can claim both taper relief and an indexation allowance, normally the indexation allowance is applied first to your gain, to be followed by the appropriate taper relief reduction.

Obtaining further relief from CGT

If part or all of your property was at any time your home, you may qualify for further relief on all or part of your CGT bill. The amount of relief you receive will depend on:

◆ how long you let all or part of your property
◆ how much of your home you let, if you were a resident landlord
◆ whether the letting took place within the last three years of ownership.

The terms under which such relief may be applied are defined under the Inland Revenue's:

- private residence relief
- lettings relief.

Further information can be found in Inland Revenue leaflets IR87 and CGT1.

Filling in your tax return form

If you believe you need to declare a chargeable gain or allowable loss to the Inland Revenue, you will need to fill in the section called Capital Gains in your tax return form, or request the supplementary pages booklet, *Capital Gains*. Notes on how to fill in your capital gains tax details will accompany the form and should be read carefully *before* starting to put figures in the boxes provided. Additional helpsheets and leaflets are available on request from the Inland Revenue.

There are stiff penalties for late receipt of tax return forms. Be careful you lodge your return in good time.

QUESTIONS AND ANSWERS

When the freezer in my rented flat broke down, I found it more cost effective to replace rather than repair. I subsequently sold the old freezer to a dealer for spares. Does the small amount I got for the old freezer count as income?

Not as income. But when you claim the cost of replacing the freezer as an allowable expense, you should deduct the sum you received on the disposal of the old freezer from the cost of the replacement.

Can I still claim a 10 per cent wear and tear allowance as usual, even though I have hardly had to spend anything on repairs this tax year?

Yes. Opting for this allowance means you are entitled to claim it every year, no matter what your actual expenditure was.

In determining my liability to CGT, does the cost of my extension attract an indexation allowance as well as the purchase price of my house?

Yes. But you must use a different indexation factor, one based on the RPI at the time the extension was complete and payment made. The costs of acquiring your property, solicitor's fees, stamp duty, etc may also be taken into account when calculating an indexation allowance deduction.

OBTAINING FURTHER INFORMATION AND ADVICE

Assessing your tax liability is an important and often tricky process. You may decide to seek further information or professional advice in this field. The sources available to you are:

- your local tax office
- Inland Revenue leaflets
- specialist books and magazines
- your bank manager
- your accountant
- a specialist tax advisory firm.

Choosing a tax adviser

When selecting a tax adviser, ask questions to ensure you get the service you want:

◆ Are you experienced in tax regulations relating to rental income?

◆ What choice of services can you offer?

◆ Would you help me complete my tax return form, if I wanted this service?

◆ What is your charging structure?

◆ How long will you take to deal with my case?

Check out a few different sources before settling on the adviser which suits you best. A recommendation is always valuable. Any adviser will need a clear picture of your whole financial situation before he or she can offer the best advice, so be prepared to give full details.

Good advice has the potential to reduce your tax bill significantly.

SUMMARY

◆ Be aware of the two taxes, income tax and capital gains tax.

◆ Obtain relevant Inland Revenue leaflets and read them.

◆ Consider how income tax will affect you.

◆ Consider how capital gains tax will affect you.

◆ Know where to seek further information.

- Decide if you need professional advice.

- Choose a tax adviser carefully using a recommendation where possible.

- Keep all records of rent and monies received and expenses and costs incurred.

- Complete a Tax Return Form (including the Land and Property booklet).

Glossary

Accommodation officer. Person employed by a university, college or company to co-ordinate the provision of accommodation for their students or personnel.

Capital gains tax (CGT). A tax levied on profit from the sale of a property (and other assets) and subject to many rules, variations, exemptions and allowances laid out by the Inland Revenue.

Capital profit. Financial gain on the intrinsic value of a property.

Company let. Rather than letting to an individual, a company can take on the tenancy of a property.

Conveyancing. The legal processes involved in buying and selling property.

Council tax. A tax levied by the local authority and payable per property. Usually, when a property is self-contained, the tenant is directly responsible for council tax, otherwise the landlord is normally responsible.

Deposit. A sum of money paid by the tenant at the start of a tenancy and held by the landlord, to be used at the end of a tenancy to pay for damage to the property by the tenant or bills left unpaid by the tenant. The exact terms of the deposit should be set out in the lease document. Monies remaining from the deposit after deductions are reimbursed to the tenant.

Downtime. Any period when a property is not producing income.

Factoring. Service provided by a letting agent which usually encompasses most of the letting workload.

Grant funding. Money available towards the costs of certain property improvements, administered by the local authority and subject to qualifying conditions, often including means-testing.

Guarantor. One who guarantees the rent payment of a tenant.

Income profit. Financial gain from receiving rent. Expenses must be subtracted from rent received in assessing income profit.

Income tax. A tax levied on income profit and subject to many rules, variations, exemptions and allowances laid out by the Inland Revenue.

Indexation. An allowance granted in determining liability to capital gains tax, geared to compensate for the general trend of inflationary price rises up to April 1998.

Insurance. A way of protecting property, contents and rental income by paying for a policy.

Inventory. A detailed list of the contents of a property.

Landlord. Person who allows use of his property by another in exchange for rent and subject to conditions set out in an agreement.

Lease. An agreement between landlord and tenant setting out the terms and conditions of the deal.

Letting agent. A person or company engaged to perform, on behalf of a landlord, some or most of his letting duties in return for payment.

Multiple occupation. When tenants with separate lease agreements occupy parts of a single property, often sharing certain facilities.

Reference. A testimonial to the character or financial standing of an individual or company and/or an assessment of their suitability.

Renovate. To improve a sub-standard or unsuitable property by performing work on it.

Rent. Payment for the use of a property.

Rent-a-room scheme. A system which offers attractive tax relief on rooms rented within the landlord's home, subject to certain qualifying terms.

Resident landlord. Someone who lives in the same premises as his tenant.

Self-contained. A complete unit, sharing no primary facilities.

Squatter. Someone who gains entry to a vacant property without permission and with the intention of settling there.

Stamp duty. A tax levied on property purchases and on the notification of tenancy agreements.

Subletting. A tenant sublets by reassigning part or all of his rented property to another for rent.

Taper Relief. An Inland Revenue relief on CGT based on the principle that the longer a property is owned, the less tax is paid. Only available from April 1998.

Ten per cent wear and tear. An allowance granted in determining liability to income tax, geared to compensate for repair and maintenance of furnishings.

Tenancy. Occupancy of a property by a tenant governed by a set of agreed terms and conditions.

Tenant. One who holds property on rent from a landlord.

Viewing. When a property on offer is shown to an interested party.

Yield. The ratio of the income profit against the capital value of the property given as a percentage figure. Yield is an indication of the return a property can produce.

Further Reading

LEGAL MATTERS

Scottish Law of Leases: An Introduction, Angus McAllister (Tottel Publishing, 2002, 3rd edition).

See You in Court! How to Conduct Your Own Case in the Small Claims Court, Anthony Reeves (Elliot Right Way Books, 1999). Note: applies to England and Wales only.

Small Claims Handbook, W. Cowan and H. Ervine (W. Green & Son, 2003). Note: applies to Scotland only.

A Straightforward Guide to Your Rights as a Private Tenant, Roger Sprotson (Straightforward Publishing, 2001, 4th edition).

The Which? Guide to Renting and Letting, Peter Wilde and Paul Butt (Which? Books, 2002, revised edition).

Free issue publications from the Scottish Executive online at www.scotland.gov.uk/housing/leaflets

Assured Tenancies in Scotland – Your Rights and Responsibilities. A guide for Private Landlords and Tenants.

Rent Assessment Committees in Scotland. A Guide for Landlords and Tenants of Assured and Short Assured Tenancies.

BUYING AND SELLING

Beating the Property Clock, Ajay Ahuja (How To Books, 2004).

Buying a House, Adam Walker (How To Books, 2001).

Buying Bargains at Property Auctions, Howard R. Gooddie (Lawpack Publishing Ltd, 2003).

How to Be Your Own Estate Agent, Tony Booth (How To Books, 2005).

PERSONAL SKILLS

Tough Taking: How to Handle Awkward Situations, David M. Martin (Financial Times Prentice Hall, 1997, revised edition).

TAXATION

Free issue publications from the Inland Revenue (tel: 0845 9000 404) or online at www.inlandrevenue.gov.uk

Capital gains tax. An introduction (Inland Revenue Publication CGT1).

Capital gains tax. A quick guide (Inland Revenue Publication CGT/FS1).

Letting and your home. Includes the 'Rent-a-Room' scheme and letting your previous home (Inland Revenue Publication IR87).

Non-resident landlords, their agents and tenants (Inland Revenue Publication IR140).

Putting things right. How to complain (Inland Revenue Publication COP1).

Taxation of rents. A guide to property income (Inland Revenue Publication IR150).

Stamp duty land tax

A quick guide to buying property (Inland Revenue Publication SD2).

A guide to leases (Inland Revenue Publication SD3).

Useful Addresses

The Association of Residential Letting Agents (ARLA), ARLA Administration, Maple House, 53–55 Woodside Road, Amersham, Buckinghamshire HP6 6AA. Tel: 0845 3455752. Web site: www.arla.co.uk

The Council for Registered Gas Installers (CORGI), 1 Elmwood, Chineham Business Park, Crockford Lane, Basingstoke, Hants RG24 6WG. Tel: (0870) 4012200. Web site: www.corgi-gas-safety.com

Federation of Master Builders, Gordon Fisher House, 14–15 Great James Street, London WC1N 3DP. Tel: (020) 7242 7583. Web site: www.fmb.org.uk

The Centre for Non-Residents, St John's House, Merton Road, Bootle, Merseyside L69 9BB. Tel: (0151) 472 6208. Web site: www.inlandrevenue.gov.uk. A branch of the Inland Revenue dealing with the taxation of rental income earned by landlords resident outside the UK.

The Stationery Office: St Crispins, Duke Street, Norwich NR3 1PD. Tel: (0870) 600 5522. Web site: www.tso.co.uk. Supplier of copies of government regulations.

Useful Web Sites

www.arla.co.uk

Well laid out web site of The Association of Residential Letting Agents. Supplies useful information and the opportunity to download free leaflets. Lists registered letting agents in your area.

www.tso.co.uk

Suppliers of a wide range of documentation inlcuding government publications.

www.corgi-gas-safety.com

The web site of the Council for Registered Gas Installers. Lists registered agents within your area.

www.fmb.org.uk

The web site of The Federation of Master Builders. Lists registered builders in your area.

www.house.co.uk

The web site of British Gas. Provides outline of landlord's statutory requirements with regard to gas servicing and certification. Contact details supplied including an on-line registration facility.

www.howtobooks.co.uk

The web site of How To Books. Lists publications available and offers a discounted on-line ordering service.

www.inlandrevenue.gov.uk

Extensive, well laid out web site of the Inland Revenue. Detailed information and leaflets can be accessed and downloaded free of charge.

www.landlords.org.uk

The web site of The National Landlords' Association which offers a journal, advice line, information sheets and tenancy documentation to its members.

www.odpm.gov.uk

Government web site providing up-to-date statistics on

house prices.

www.rla.org.uk

The web site of The Residential Landlords Association. Offers members a news magazine, training, advice, tenant credit checks, landlord insurance, etc.

www.scotland.gov.uk

The web site of the Scottish Executive. Provides very readable guidelines on a Landlord's rights and responsibilities under Scottish law.

Index